STRANGE WAR, STRANGE STRATEGY

To: Sue Mason
with warm personal
regards and best
wishes Lew Walt

9/19/70

Strange War, Strange Strategy

A GENERAL'S REPORT ON VIETNAM

Lewis W. Walt

GENERAL, U.S. MARINE CORPS

INTRODUCTION BY LYNDON B. JOHNSON

Funk & Wagnalls

NEW YORK

To all those Americans who have supported the cause of freedom in South Vietnam; to those who have so gallantly sacrificed their lives or well-being on the battlefields; to the families who have suffered the loss of loved ones; to those who have shouldered the sorrow and compassion for the wounded and ill; to the men whose names are still listed under the tragic designation of "missing in action" or "prisoners of war" and their families, this book is dedicated with deep respect.

Contents

Introduction

BY LYNDON B. JOHNSON

Only a few men are qualified to write about the war in Vietnam on the basis of both command responsibility and long first-hand experience. Even fewer are aware of both the military problems and the economic, political, and social forces at work in this most complicated of all our wars. Gen. Lewis W. Walt has those qualifications, and he has drawn on them in writing this book.

I remember well my first talk with General Walt about Vietnam. He had gone out in May 1965 to take command of Marine units that had landed in the northern part of South Vietnam to protect our airbases and other installations. A few months later their mission was expanded to include active combat against the Viet Cong and North Vietnamese who were threatening to take over the entire country by force.

In February 1966 General Walt returned to Washington for consultation. On the 25th of that month, he came to see me at the White House. I can still see him walking firmly across to my desk in the Oval Office—the square jaw and steady eyes; the shoulders broad as a fullback's; the straight back of the military professional; the strong, calloused hands of a man who likes to use them, and does. In every way, he was a "Marine's Marine," as they say in the Corps.

Introduction

We talked for nearly two hours. He told me in crisp detail what was happening, how things looked, how our men were doing in a kind of war some people had argued they never could fight effectively. He told me a great many other things, too. He described the South Vietnamese Army—its strength and weaknesses. Above all, he talked with feeling and compassion about the Vietnamese people and what they were going through—the terror imposed by the communist forces; the pain they felt when their rice was confiscated and their sons were dragged away to fight; the torture and murders that were the penalty for failing to do what the Viet Cong demanded.

He also told me what his Marines and our other fighting men were doing to help the people. They were building schools and dispensaries in nearby villages. Medical corpsmen were going out during their off-duty hours to give inoculations against disease, to treat the festering sores of young and old, and to relieve the pain of the suffering. Many young Marines were living in villages with local defense forces, helping to protect the people against the terror and taxation of a ruthless, demanding enemy.

Here was a rugged Marine general fighting a tough and exhausting war. Yet he showed more real feeling, more sensitivity for the people who were its victims, than almost anyone I knew. Much of what he told me that day in the White House, and on numerous later occasions, is in these pages. But there is a great deal more.

There is war, of course—descriptions of major engagements and small unit actions as only a perceptive veteran of thirty-five years of military service can recount them. But this book transcends the battlefield. It describes many events and programs that never got into our newspapers. They were not dramatic or destructive. It shows young Americans in the midst of war's horrors yet keeping their humanity, their loyalty to each

Introduction

other and to their country, and most important, their compassion for the men, women, and children around them.

This book helps explain in clear terms why men like General Walt and the Marines and all our fighting forces have managed thus far to help keep 17 million Vietnamese free and masters of their own future. And it exposes the real nature of a brutal communist enemy who, because of his ambition and his aggression, has brought so much suffering to so many for so long. This is something every young American should know before he is tempted to walk down the street following the flag of that enemy whose leaders and supporters seek to conquer ever more territory by aggression.

The Marine Corps has traditionally been in the forefront when aggression had to be faced and beaten back, when the interests of our country had to be protected. Its role in Vietnam is but the most recent chapter in a glorious history of gallantly protecting our friends and ourselves. Most Americans, I know, share my deep admiration and gratitude for what this brave corps of men has done, is doing, and will continue to do to make this country safe—even though a few of our citizens loudly scorn those who protect them.

The majority of Americans who support what our country has been trying to do in Southeast Asia in the past decade—and those who oppose that policy—will both come away from reading this book with a clearer picture of what this conflict is all about. And that can only be to the good.

STRANGE WAR, STRANGE STRATEGY

DMZ

Cam Lo
Con Thien
Khe Sanh
Quang Tri
Province
Dong Ha

Hue
Phu Bai

Thua Thien
Province

I CORPS AREA

(U.S. MARINES)

Danang

Quang Nam Province

Quang Tin
Province
Chu Lai

Quang Ngai
Province

REPUBLIC OF

VIETNAM

⊛ SAIGON

I

Turnabout

In the first months of 1965 press dispatches from Vietnam drew a grim picture of impending calamity. They merely confirmed reports of a likely communist takeover reaching Washington from American advisors in the country and urgent pleas for military help from the government in Saigon. Typical of the alarming tidings was a story that appeared on our newsstands on March 8. It had been written a few days before in Danang, the second largest city in the Republic of Vietnam:

> Travel today up the long, narrow waist of central Vietnam —north from Saigon to the seventeenth parallel—and you reach this unmistakable conclusion:
>
> The makings of a military disaster for the U.S. and South Vietnam are starting to fall into place here with a major communist offensive becoming possible any time the Red leaders are willing to pay the price.
>
> Everywhere along this central Vietnamese Corridor, with only a few exceptions, I saw Government forces on the defensive.
>
> Communist forces are employing the same strategy they used against the French in leading up to the disaster at

Turnabout

Dienbienphu. They are chopping each Province off, cutting its land communications with its neighbors, terrorizing its local population.

South Vietnamese troops and their U.S. advisors, while fighting bravely in many areas, have no overall strategy except to try to keep their lines of communication open. . . .*

On that same day in 1965 the first of many thousands of United States Marines were landing in the Republic of Vietnam. These men encountered more than the impending military disaster so accurately reported in their homeland: they also encountered the task of preventing it.

From a short time after the initial American landings to the summer of 1967 I commanded the Marines in Vietnam. Since then, as Assistant Commandant of the U. S. Marine Corps, I have been in a position to follow and assess the war from a national level, assisted by a professional staff, and have revisited Vietnam at every opportunity. I have seen, from that first bleak spring of 1965, the Viet Cong virtually destroyed, reduced to hiding in the hills or confined to random and indiscriminate terrorism; the vast majority of the people loyal to and under the effective protection of the government and armed forces of the Republic of Vietnam. I have seen the Viet Cong movement lose all of its characteristics as a local, popular movement and degenerate into overt invasion of regular forces from the north. I have seen a nation revitalized with a determination to remain free, its paralysis of fear replaced with confidence and action.

When the Vietnamese people asked for our help, they had already endured a virtually uninterrupted war for two decades. Still struggling to recover from the devastation of World War II, their country was ravaged again by the long and agonizing

---

* Sol Sanders, "I Saw the Making of a Disaster in Vietnam," *U.S. News & World Report,* March 8, 1965.

conflict between the forces of France and the anticolonial Viet Minh movement. Soon after the end of this Indochina War and the establishment of a northern and a southern state, the government and the people of the new Republic of Vietnam came under systematic attack from the Vietnamese communists—the Viet Cong. Organized groups of terrorists appeared in the cities and villages, armed from caches of weapons and ammunition hidden during the previous years of conflict. Men born in the south, after being indoctrinated and trained in the north, were sent back to their native hamlets; their assignment was to wreck the very institutions and facilities that held the promise of stabilization for their own people: schools and local government, doctors and nurses, roads, railroads, and bridges.

The communist enemy was strong and determined. He spread his influence throughout the country, supplied and assisted from neighboring states over a network of well-developed roads and trails. By 1965 the armed forces of the Republic of Vietnam, which had but recently come into existence, had been depleted of substantive leadership by a combination of battlefield casualties, insufficient time, and facilities inadequate for training and developing new leaders. They were demoralized by successive defeats at the hands of a cunning and merciless enemy. The American forces that entered the country were eight thousand air miles from San Francisco, without bases in or near Vietnam, exposed to a new kind of warfare, in a chaotic political and economic situation and a debilitating climate.

It was almost inconceivable that the government of the young Republic could last out the year. It was barely conceivable that even the power of the United States could restore security and confidence to a people weary of war and long tormented by terror and subversion. By June of 1967, nevertheless, convoys were running on a regular basis from just south of the Demilitarized Zone between the two new nations for over a hundred miles down the coast, through the old capital city of Hué, through Danang and Quang Ngai, past miles of villages and paddyfields with vegetable gardens in between.

The South Vietnamese government was beginning to operate under a liberal constitution, drafted by men and women selected by the people and ratified by elected representatives of the people. Many of the cities, villages, and hamlets were staffed with elected officials. By mid-1967 more than a million people had been freed from communist domination by the actions of Free World forces and their South Vietnamese allies. The Army of the Republic of Vietnam and its sister services in the Marine Corps area of Vietnam—as generally elsewhere throughout the country—were stronger, more capable, better equipped, and operating against the enemy with increased confidence and efficiency.

The Main Force units of the Viet Cong, once able to move in battalions and regiments throughout central Vietnam, had been broken up and forced into the unpopulated mountain areas or out of the country into Laos or North Vietnam. The Viet Cong guerrillas were still effective, hiding among the people, still able to harass many villages and hamlets through terror and coercion, but their control over the people was sharply diminished with the loss of Viet Cong Main Force support.

The North Vietnamese had thrown in major forces of their regular army, in an overt invasion across the Demilitarized Zone established by the Geneva Accords of 1954. This was a desperate attempt to restore the balance to the enemy side. They were met in conventional battle, and learned the bitter lesson of defeat.

Among the people vast quantities of rice were again being harvested each season without Viet Cong confiscation or taxation. Small businesses were beginning to flourish, schools were reopened, bridges and roads were restored for the free flow of goods and services between communities. Public health and sanitation agencies, vocational training, administrative services, and farmer and fisherman cooperatives were established and functioning.

The big airbase complex at Danang, the commercial port, and civilian air service were in full and unhindered operation. Not one provincial capital had been seized and held by the enemy.

In short, the dire prediction of two years earlier had been reversed. The Viet Cong had experienced the defeats, and continued to exist only as weakened auxiliaries to the regular army of North Vietnam.

During the tenure of my command, hundreds of analysts and experts visited Vietnam. Writers and reporters filed millions of words of copy. Cameras peered over the shoulders of men in battle. The world, and particularly our own people, were inundated with information and interpretation of what was happening in Vietnam.

When I returned home, I was confident that we had not only averted the expected disaster but had also turned the course of the war against the enemy. I was tremendously proud of the young Americans in Vietnam and the courage and fortitude of the Vietnamese in their fight against subjugation. I was keenly aware that over four thousand of the men under my command had given their lives in that fight and that almost seventeen thousand had been wounded. I knew, however, that this was the price we had paid to decimate the Viet Cong, to drive him away from the people and into the Laotian hills, to fight off divisions of regular North Vietnamese invaders, and to root out the "tax collectors" and terrorists who preyed upon the villagers.

Since my return, I have continued to be vitally concerned with the war in Vietnam. I have seen stability and security grow, and control by the Viet Cong reduced to a remnant of its former strength. I have seen the Republic of Vietnam become an increasingly dynamic force in Southeast Asia and achieve a solidarity that refuses to be fractured from without or within. I have shared the relief of all Americans on seeing our men begin the long voyage home, the hardest part of their task done.

I have returned to Vietnam several times, to observe again the circumstances and progress of the war. I have talked to thousands of Americans directly, and to millions more by radio and television, concerning our commitment in Vietnam and my own experiences there.

In my many discussions with our people I have been both astonished and distressed by the misconceptions so many of them hold about our own operations in Vietnam, about the Vietnamese people, the Viet Cong, and the North Vietnamese. I have also reached a growing conviction that the story of what the individual American fighting man—soldier, sailor, airman, or Marine—is doing in Vietnam has not been adequately told. Too few Americans seemed aware—and some found the fact unbelievable—that some forty-two thousand Marines and over a hundred thousand soldiers of the U. S. Army have voluntarily remained in Vietnam at the end of their tour of duty, or requested to go back to Vietnam after returning to the comfort and safety of the United States.

It is common, and proper, for generals to write for history. But that is not my intention. I am writing for the people of my own or any other country who are saddened by the war in Vietnam, who are bitter or confused as to its purpose or its outcome. For I have been saddened by this war as profoundly as any of them, and more than most; sometimes as bitter and as confused as any of them, and often more so. Moreover, there were few in the world more deeply involved in the confusion and frustration of the conflict than myself, or more broadly aware of its problems, from peasant to potentate. I sought answers desperately. Sometimes I found them in unexpected places.

Soon after I arrived in Vietnam it became obvious to me that I had neither a real understanding of the nature of the war nor any clear idea as to how to win it. I suppose that doctors feel equally forlorn when they are baffled by what is wrong with a patient, except that my "patient" was an entire countryside, with the lives of thousands resting on my judgments. Searching for understanding, I went among the people, the masses whose faces show the anguish and tragedy of war.

Twelve miles north of Danang there was a small hamlet that had been occupied by the Viet Cong until only recently, when our expanding patrols clashed with them and drove them away. Here were people who had lived through French colonialism, then communist occupation, and were now reclaimed by a government in Saigon, through American action.

I talked with an elderly couple, both in their seventies, who had lived in that hamlet all their lives, whose once large family had been reduced by war to one small grandchild; two old people of enormous dignity, calm, and patient wisdom. What they told me was sufficiently moving to record and report in my own words, trying to retain the sincerity and deep feeling with which they spoke:

It wasn't too bad prior to the Viet Cong takeover, except the people in the hamlets and villages had no prestige and they were taxed heavily. It is good for a man and a woman to see life grow better as the years pass, knowing that their children will not have a way as hard as their own has been, but no progress was being made toward a better way of life.

The Viet Minh came in 1952 and 1953, and it seemed to be good. They came as friends and neighbors, joining in the social events and participating in the local government as equals. We had confidence in them, because they had caused the French to leave and promised a chance for a better life, in freedom and independence.

But they did not keep their promises. They killed the village chief and disbanded the village council, and this destroyed the village government. Later, they were no longer Viet Minh, but Vietnamese communists, and their rule was harsh.

They paused for a moment, their eyes following the little granddaughter, then continued:

The young people were taken from the village and sent north for indoctrination and training, to return as Viet Cong and to fight with the other forces to liberate the rest of Vietnam, as they said. The little school was destroyed, and the church and the market place. We were forbidden to have any assembly or organization not authorized by the Viet Cong leader in the village.

Our village is hemmed in by a river on two sides, and we have always had to cross it to visit Danang or other communities, but the Viet Cong tore down the bridges over which we used to take carts, and replaced them with one footbridge, always guarded, and we could not go over it without a written pass from the Viet Cong leader. No more than half of any family could leave the village at any one time, so there would always be hostages left behind if any of us disobeyed them or failed to return.

The Viet Cong taxes were heavy, up to half of what we produced, and two days each week we had to do work assigned by the Viet Cong: building fortifications or carrying supplies.

There were eight hundred of us in the village, and only twenty-five Viet Cong, but they were armed and we were not, and they were organized and we were not, and the way was hard.

And now your people have come, and we do not know how things will be, but our desires are the same. We would like to be independent and free to live our life in the way we choose, and most of all we would like to see a better life than we have known, for our grandchild, who is all that is left to us, and for the children of the others, if they remain.

In each of the hamlets, the words of the people were the same. I began to understand the war a little better.

For two years after that, we fought a manysided battle: against the Viet Cong; later, against the regular army of North Vietnam; against poverty and disease, want and hopelessness; and always against fear, terror, and coercion.

The price paid by the Vietnamese people for "liberation" as brought to them by the Viet Cong is almost impossible for an American to conceive. Only those who have seen it can grasp its dimensions and its horror.

2

The Price of "Liberation"

The hamlet of Tri Binh was several miles south of Chu Lai. It was in an area conceded to the Viet Cong during the grim spring of 1965, and later reclaimed by the Republic of Vietnam as the enemy fled, or went underground, to avoid the security patrols expanding outward from the U.S. Marine airbase at Chu Lai.

The people of Tri Binh were not unhappy at the change. Compared with the severity of Viet Cong control, life under the Saigon government was pleasant. There was a return to the old cycle of birth, marriage, and death, marked with the ceremonies traditional for a thousand years. Family groups were reunited, there was more and better food, opportunity to visit other hamlets for barter, to see acquaintances and relatives.

The hamlet chief was an energetic young man, efficient, dedicated, and courageous. Working with both the government and the Americans, he performed wonders for his people: the school was restored and education for the children resumed; a market place was built, with cover from the sun and a clean concrete floor; a medical team from the Marine base visited each week to treat the ill; the hamlet well was improved with

The Price of "Liberation"

bricks and mortar. A section of abandoned paddy was replanted with rice, the field work rotated among all the families, the harvest used both as a food reserve and a communal method of tax payment to avoid assessment on each family.

The Republic of Vietnam's red and yellow flag was raised each day, proclaiming loyalty to the government. Across the narrow street was a handmade banner: "What have the Viet Cong done for you?"

The hamlet chief met weekly with the heads of family groups, elders chosen by the people. With them he worked out the problems of the community, the needs and complaints of the people. His wife helped with a women's committee, and he had the extra assistance of a keen young man in his teens, who had enthusiastically formed a youth group.

Marine patrols enjoyed passing through Tri Binh. The health and general well-being of the villagers were apparent. Their greetings were cheery, and they pointed to each new improvement with obvious pride. Sometimes a patrol would double back toward Tri Binh before nightfall and place an ambush on a nearby road or trail during the curfew hours. From their positions they would watch the cookfires gradually gutter out in the peaceful hamlet as the long night began. The Viet Cong watched, too, with patient eyes, and did not come at night, but came instead in the bright morning hours of the last day of 1965.

Up early, the hamlet chief had given instructions to the youth leader and walked off toward Chu Lai to obtain material for a new project. He was found later that morning, on the road. He had been shot three times in the back and a *coup de grâce* had been fired into the base of his skull as he lay face downward in the dust. There were the footprints of two men in the nearby drainage ditch and the empty shells of their Chinese-made weapons.

The Price of "Liberation"

The hamlet was stunned and sad. A new hamlet chief, if sent in by the government, would be a stranger, and they did not like strangers in their midst. Yet none of the elders was willing to assume leadership of the community, with the hamlet chief's blood still moist on the road. They feared the Viet Cong and also feared the end of a happy, prosperous hamlet life. Only one retained the courage to act—the teen-age youth leader.

He had received instructions from the hamlet chief only moments before he died. While others sat in mute despair, the young man went forward with the work of the hamlet. He walked down the lonely road to Chu Lai and obtained the needed supplies in the name of the murdered chief. In a few days the people found themselves with a new leader—the youngster who seemed to know what to do and how to do it. The elders met with him as they had met with the hamlet chief and listened to his young, dynamic ideas as if he were also an elder. The hamlet continued to prosper, the Republic's flag was flown each morning, the banner still hung across the street, asking "What have the Viet Cong done for you?"

And again in broad daylight two Viet Cong walked into the hamlet to the home of the new leader, led him to where his chief had died, and shot him to death there on the road. He had led his people for the last twenty-six days of his young life. He was killed by men who called themselves the *Mat Tran Dan-toc Giai-phong Mien-Nam*—National Liberation Front of South Vietnam.

Since 1965 this "liberation" has meant the assassination or kidnapping of over ninety thousand Vietnamese civilians. The tragedy of Tri Binh has been suffered by hundreds of other hamlets. With few exceptions, the victims represented the leadership of the country: hamlet and village chiefs, teachers, nurses, agriculturists, and public health workers—the people who make government work at the local level. It is difficult for

The Price of "Liberation"

Americans to realize the impact of such a selective elimination of leadership and administrative talent on a small and newly independent country formerly governed by white Europeans.

We must occasionally remind ourselves that the population of twelve South Vietnams would be less than our own by many millions. To South Vietnam, the loss of ninety thousand key people is equivalent to the United States losing over a million municipal, county, state, and Federal employees. Such has been the price of "liberation" by the Viet Cong.

Until the deaths of John F. Kennedy, Martin Luther King, Jr., and Robert F. Kennedy, it may have appeared to some Americans that a government was delinquent to permit the slaughter of its leaders, or that the people themselves either approved or were apathetic toward their elimination. Our own tragedies have brought a better understanding.

In 1965, when I first arrived, there were two hundred thousand Viet Cong in the Republic of Vietnam. Not one of these was less dangerous than the men who gunned down our own leaders. Moreover, they were dangerous not only to the national leaders but also to anyone, however humble, who evidenced love for his people, loyalty to his government, or the slightest disagreement with communist rule. Worse, the Viet Cong were capable of incredibly cruel torture as well as the swift sniper bullet from a hiding place. They were capable of attacking a well-guarded man through his wife and children, his sister or mother, to force him to their service. The Viet Cong were at war with their own people, long before we entered Vietnam, and had ruthlessly brought war's anguish to millions of Vietnamese.

Although the volume of reporting, analysis, and debate on Vietnam is greater than for any previous war, most Americans seem quite unclear as to who and what the Viet Cong is. A typical impression is that of a cunning and experienced guerrilla fighter; a patriot fighting to unify his country, eject foreign foes, eliminate a corrupt and inefficient government. We who have fought him know this man, too. It is the business of a soldier to know his enemy, without illusion. After four years we now know him well.

With rare exceptions he is a young man—fourteen to twenty-five years old. At the most, he was not over ten years old when the French were defeated at Dienbienphu. Some 40 per cent of the Viet Cong are conscripts, boys taken from villages at the point of a gun. Very few have any ideological reason for fighting. But a substantial number—and this is enormously important to us—are fighting as a result of deep indoctrination, relentless propaganda, the incessant repetition of ideas and slogans essential to the communist system. They fight for what their minds have been molded to regard as social justice and opportunity, and against what they have been conditioned to regard as evil.

The system for which these young men give their lives is also less than clear to the American people. It is almost impossible for an American who has not directly encountered it to visualize such brutal efficiency as Asian communism. The people of Asia are learning, in increasing segments, and they recite their lessons with their feet whenever they are given the opportunity.

We should take closer note of the twenty-two thousand Chinese and North Korean soldiers, some two-thirds of all the prisoners of war, who refused to return to their communist homelands after the Korean war; the eight hundred thousand Vietnamese who fled south from the rule of Ho Chi Minh at the end of the first Indochina War. Then we would be less surprised at the millions of people who have fled Viet Cong control since 1965.

Partly, the reason for these vast exoduses is provided by the communist leaders themselves:

The Price of "Liberation"

HOANG VAN AN: The Party has been guided by the principle that it is better to kill ten innocent people than to let one enemy escape.*

GEN. VO NGUYEN GIAP: Every minute, hundreds of thousands of people die all over the world. The life or death of thousands of human beings, even if they are compatriots, represents really very little.†

CHAIRMAN MAO TSE-TUNG: The seizure of power by armed force, the settlement of the issue by war, is the central task and the highest form of revolution. This Marxist-Leninist principle of revolution holds universally, for China and for all other countries.‡

Even more clearly, the reason vast numbers of people flee communism is provided by observation of its practice in Southeast Asia. Through all the cant and argument, this is plain: the Viet Cong deny the people individual dignity, religious freedom, cohesive family life, and the ownership of private property—the very things the Vietnamese traditionally most cherish.

Under the Viet Cong the individual is meaningless except for his contribution to the faceless state miscalled "the people." He is expected—and forced—to abuse himself by self-criticism; to condemn and disown, as a duty, his friends and relatives; to live and work only for the Party, to think only through the Party and its leaders.

The family unit is destroyed by self and mutual incrimination, social organization of the community into age and sex groups for more "disciplined" control, the grinding loads of

* *From Colonialism to Communism* (London: Pall Mall).
† Quoted by Dr. Bernard Fall in *Viet-Nam Witness* (New York: Praeger).
‡ Peking International Service English-language Broadcast, July 10, 1963.

extra labor, and the constant meetings and brainwashing sessions that supplant family life.

Religion, the very belief in a deity, is condemned as superstition, and believers are discriminated against and persecuted. The little society in which most Vietnamese live—the hamlet and village—is turned into a complex of Communist Party pressure groups and informers, each trying to survive by demonstrating his Party loyalty, each being denounced by his neighbors. Children are turned against their parents, husbands against their wives, wives against their husbands.

Private ownership is almost totally eliminated. In the world of the Viet Cong everything belongs to the dictatorship posing as "the people." The peasant uses his hoe or his water buffalo only by the sufferance of the state. The needs of the Party supersede any requirement or preference of the individual or the family. The farmer is assigned a plot of land to till, only to look on helplessly as all of the grain is confiscated when it ripens.

I have seen communities leave their homes, their buffalo, and their standing grain at the first opportunity to escape this frightful existence. One cluster of peasants begged to be shot by our men if we could not evacuate them, preferring death to continued Viet Cong control. Farmers have pleaded with us to protect them as they harvested their rice, knowing that otherwise they would be destitute after the Viet Cong confiscation.

In numerous areas of Vietnam, where the Viet Cong had been relatively undisturbed for many years—primarily sections of the coast between major towns—we found less severity. Hamlets and villages were tidy and well run, the people were adapted to government by the communists, as they would have adapted to any authority, meeting its demands while salvaging what normal life they could under the circumstances. Where Viet Cong control was absolute, it was superficially reasonable and often appeared mild, but the fundamental policies were still enforced: the state took precedence over the individual

The Price of "Liberation"

and his family; each person possessed some private property only by its sufferance.

But where there was an opportunity for the people to compare life under the Viet Cong to that under the government of the Republic of Vietnam, pressures on the people were intensified. Much of the destruction of public works such as roads, bridges, railroads, and causeways so common throughout Vietnam was effected by the Viet Cong not so much for military reasons as for isolation of the people from other communities. As in Berlin and Hong Kong, Korea and Cuba, direct comparison of systems is odious to communist regimes.

Where the people were provided a choice between systems —the chance to escape Viet Cong control—coercion, terrorism, and reprisal were most ruthless. This was the most terrible part of the terrible war. The most cruel acts, the most wanton disregard for human life, occurred on the constantly expanding boundaries between the two systems.

The men who wear uniforms, even the black pajamas of the Viet Cong, have little reason to be surprised at the human cost of war. It has been the lot of the soldier since the days of Joshua to risk, and perhaps lose, his life in battle. It has also been the lot of the unarmed populace to be victims of the battle, sometimes inadvertently and all too often deliberately. But even in the most terrible battles, when "they smote them so that they let none of them remain or escape," the cruelty of men has been something less than deliberate maiming of children, random killing of anyone who happens by, reversion to the savagery of death by torture—which are the specific methods of the Viet Cong.

One day there was a bus rolling along at a good pace from Quang Ngai to Danang, filled with the common people of Vietnam. Just south of Danang there is a fork in the road, one way leading inland and the other bearing to the right into the city itself. With traffic from three directions, many vehicles stop to pick up people using the juncture as a transfer point. It is a rather pleasant place, with a row of acacia trees for shade and the colorful vehicles streaming by, some red and yellow, some blue and white, most of them packed with passengers.

This bus was red and yellow, and it stopped to discharge one man, then pulled away under the broad arch of the trees. From an overhanging limb a young Vietnamese tossed a container of gasoline at the vehicle below. The container burst, spilling the liquid through the open windows and splashing it onto the roof of the bus. Perhaps, some thought, it was the practical joke of schoolboys hidden in the bushes alongside the road. They may have been angered because their clothes would be stained and the vegetables in their woven baskets ruined. Perhaps—we shall never know—someone in the bus called for the driver to stop; and, alerted by the commotion to his rear, he moved to put on the brakes. The bus traveled only a few feet from its stop, just to the next tree, where a second young man perched overhead threw a lighted torch onto the fuel-soaked people below.

Quickly the two vandals dropped from the trees and ran. The bus screeched to a halt, yellow flame gushing. The two running figures could hear the screams and knew they had done their task well. Moments later, the muffled explosion and smudge of black smoke billowing skyward no doubt had given them and their leaders great satisfaction. More than twenty of their own Vietnamese people were horribly burned.

I visited these pathetic victims in the civilian hospital at Danang. Normally, there are sounds in a hospital ward: a moan, a rustling of bedclothes, someone talking. But here, among these crisped and tortured figures, sound seemed replaced by movement, a ghastly, silent writhing, their agony coming through the heavy sedation in ceaseless motion.

We could never find out why that one bus was chosen. It was

on a schedule of convenience, its time of arrival unpredictable. It had been delayed for some time farther south, waiting for the repair of a culvert, along with many other vehicles. It might or might not have stopped at that particular point, and not necessarily at those two trees. Its destruction was a random act of terrorism, and the target could equally have been the bus before or the one after. The atrocity was as indiscriminate as the Viet Cong land mines, placed upon the road to blow up vehicles, whether a bus full of children or a truckload of soldiers. The objective is the same: terror.

Then there is discriminate terror. I recall vividly a gruesome Viet Cong propaganda picture shown to me. The caption, roughly translated, read: "The people take revenge on a corrupt Saigon puppet." It showed a crowd of villagers looking on as several of their number beat a mutilated body. Within hours after the picture was taken, while the body still lay in the village market place, I walked its streets and heard what had happened from a terrified and sorrowing people.

The village chief had been energetic and popular, and the village had thrived under his leadership. The Viet Cong had come in the early evening and the people had been assembled in the market place. The village chief and his family—a wife and two children—were marched, hands tied behind their backs, to the center of the small open area. One of the Viet Cong read a statement setting forth the official's alleged acts "against the people." Listening, the villagers turned their heads in amazement; this was not the village chief they knew. Accusations were being made that they knew to be untrue; acts that had brought them a better way of life were branded "crimes"; a man they had come to respect as a leader and an example was labeled "traitor."

As a dozen armed Viet Cong leveled their submachine guns on the crowd, sentence was pronounced: death for the chief and his family. Some might have surged forward to defend him; others might have turned their faces to avoid the scene; but all were held in place by the submachine guns.

As the Viet Cong held him, the once proud village chief turned into a raging, half-crazed father as he watched his two children mutilated to death; then into a sobbing, broken husband as his wife died under their bayonets; then, with no will or strength left to resist or protest, he stood as the red and yellow Vietnamese flag that had flown over the village was wrapped about his head, soaked in kerosene, and ignited. The terrorized villagers were given clubs and ordered to beat his lifeless form. As their cudgels rose and fell, flashbulbs glittered and cameras clicked so the world could be privileged to observe "the people" destroying another "traitor."

I had seen a lot of war before Vietnam, but never such war directed at unarmed civilians or projected by the random slaughter of innocents. It was war untempered by any mercy; worse, the good, the kind, the most helpless, were primary targets in this war.

What of Nguyen Thich, a poor farmer, an elder in a hamlet between Danang and our base at Chu Lai, who asked the Viet Cong how they could talk of liberation when they terrorized the people? Their answer was to beat him to death and leave his body in the village market place as a lesson to others.

What of a man who argued with no one and devoted his entire energies to helping the people—a man of God, a Vietnamese, who had worked three years with a group of refugees? Together, they had built their own houses, planted trees for shade, and raised a church and school. He taught the women to sew and weave straw hats, the men to barber, operate a laundry, and repair bicycles, and they prospered. And early in the morning, on May 15, 1967, the Viet Cong came to kill him. They fired high-explosive rockets through the walls of his house. We heard, and came quickly, and the Viet Cong fled

The Price of "Liberation"

into the early-morning darkness. We found the man's broken body and flew him by helicopter to the nearest doctor, but there he died of his wounds. He was a good man, a kind man, one whom the Viet Cong therefore would not permit to live.

What of a small boy, seven years old, playing happily on his way home from school one day? The Viet Cong abducted him from the road and took him into the jungle near his home. There two of them held him while a third lopped off his hands with a machete. Then they pushed him out of the jungle toward his home. His mother heard his screams and ran to pick him up. I was there, and I watched as she carried him into the village, blood staining her clothes. A crude sign, hung around the boy's neck, warned: "This, or worse, if you or your neighbors go to the voting place on Election Day!"

Such incidents were not confined to the Marine Corps areas of Vietnam; they permeated the country.

It has been largely forgotten that the beginning of the Viet Cong attacks against the Republic of Vietnam, more than ten years ago, included the vicious extermination of unarmed malaria control teams. Americans find it difficult to understand that discrediting the government should be more important to the communists than freeing the people from a debilitating and often fatal disease. In the modern world there is no reason why the Vietnamese need suffer malaria—except for the Viet Cong, who have prevented its eradication for political purposes.

How can we understand the premeditated murder of missionaries selflessly devoting themselves to the care of Vietnamese lepers? Yet the Viet Cong attacked the leprosarium at Ban Me Thuot, massacred the staff (unarmed men and women), and totally destroyed the buildings. Two thousand patients, suffering from the dread and disfiguring disease, were left without care.

Refugees, the tragic backwash of every war, are another common target of Viet Cong attack. So are the Montagnards,

primitive tribes in the hill country, subjected to Viet Cong conscription, confiscation, impressment as beasts of burden, or terrible reprisals.

Dak Son was a Montagnard village that refused to cooper-
ate. It was burned to the ground. The Viet Cong moved
through the village for an hour with submachine guns and
flamethrowers. They killed over two hundred of the Montagnards—in burning huts, in tunnels and caves dug as shelters,
in the open and in the jungle. They left an unforgettable scene:
blackened bodies in front of ruined homes; two children fused
together by a flamethrower as they clutched each other in terror; a father mourning his twelve dead children.

The Vietnamese people have been suffering these horrors
since the 1950s. I saw only two years of them: a pregnant girl,
only nineteen, beaten and shot when she would not join the
Viet Cong; whole villages demolished by gasoline and torch; a
fifteen-year-old girl tortured and beheaded by her own brother
and two other Viet Cong; tongues cut out; death by disembow-
eling, by bamboo splinters in the scrotum, by a lance through
the ears, by castration; eyes gouged out of their sockets;
women and children stabbed to death with bayonets.

Such is Vietnamese communism as I knew it, and I knew far
less than did the people who were its victims. I have heard
cynics discount the mass of refugees as people escaping only
from American bombs and napalm. I have seen our own youth
parading the American streets under the Viet Cong flag. But
those not insulated from the Viet Cong by eight thousand miles
know them better than to bear their banner. We know also that
the Viet Cong are losing the people of Vietnam and that they
have good reason to fear the people.

Our own men, too, have been victims of the communist strategy of terror. For two years I saw them exposed to the horrors
of guerrilla warfare and saw them bear up under it. I watched
their fortitude and restraint with increasing admiration, affec-

The Price of "Liberation"

tion, and respect. I saw them die, and I saw them wounded. I lived each moment of their victories and their defeats.

The American burden of the war was not borne by generals like myself or by citizens who found it difficult to understand what was happening in Vietnam. The burden was, and remains, on the young men, both enlisted and commissioned. On the one hand, they meet the enemy in close, vicious, and protracted conflict, while, on the other, they show the compassion to comfort a sick child, help rebuild a school, or assist a farmer in harvesting his crop. It is their story also I shall try to tell.

3
Strange Country, Strange War

Vietnam is a country of greens in infinite variety, from the blue-green of the mountains to the brilliant green of young rice in the paddies. It is a beautiful country, marred only by the war. It is a calm country, disturbed only by the war.

The people of Vietnam are as beautiful and calm as their land. Slight, well formed, graceful, their eyes and faces full of expression, they are a gentle people of great charm. They grow old with dignity and are buried with respect in the fields they have tilled.

Vietnam is a rich country, not in Gross National Product or fiscal reserves, but in its hills and fields, magnificent tropical forests, well-watered valleys, and vast flood-plains.

The area of Vietnam assigned to the U.S. Marines began at the Demilitarized Zone and continued south for a hundred and sixty-seven miles, as far as from New York to Baltimore, and extended from the South China Sea inland to Laos. The western border is a jumble of deeply forested mountains—cool, wet, thinly populated. Toward the coast the foothills are grassland and brush, cut by river valleys and stream beds. Along the coast itself and for several miles inland the land flattens out into the fertile alluvial plain where most of the people live and most of the rice is grown.

Another feature, obvious from both the air and the ground, is the projection of forested ridges from the mountains to the sea. These break up the populated coastal plain into segments— huge crescents of lowland separated by long arms of hill and jungle reaching toward the coast.

Our area contained five provinces—synonymous with the separate states of our own country—and was identical to the area for which the First (I) Corps of the Army of the Republic of Vietnam was responsible.

The Marines came as strangers to this land and its people.

Although it may not always seem so to the public, military forces are committed with a precise definition as to what they are intended to do. This mission may be very broad, such as seizing and holding Guadalcanal, or in detail, such as the careful definitions provided to Federal troops for their participation in a domestic disturbance. In the case of the Marines entering Vietnam, the mission was explicit and simple: Defend the airbases at Danang and Phu Bai, and provide security for building an airbase at Chu Lai. Danang was the major city in our area. Phu Bai was several miles outside of the old capital city of Hué. Chu Lai was a thinly populated stretch of coast about forty-five miles south of Danang.

Our original mission permitted only static defense around the designated airbases. We were not allowed to patrol beyond the defense areas. Our own forces were divided into three unequal parts to cover the three separated base areas. We could move between them by sea or air; overland communication was minimal and risky.

I have always felt that the individual Vietnamese at first regarded us as a return of the French with different clothes and tongue. We had to learn and remember—as the Vietnamese already knew and remembered—that the French had conquered Indochina by force as long ago as the American Civil War; that they had dominated Vietnam, Cambodia, and Laos during the same time they had assisted Maximilian to dominate Mexico; that Vietnamese resistance to the French was an expression of a proud people against Occidental colonialism.

We had to recall, too, that the original Viet Minh began as a coalition of Vietnamese nationalist resistance forces twenty-five years before our landing in 1965—the Vietnam Doc-Lap Dong-Minh; that this organization, under the guidance of Ho Chi Minh, had set up a provisional Vietnamese government upon the surrender of Japan in 1945.

Even those of us who were active at the end of World War II needed an effort of memory to recall that British Commonwealth and Chinese troops had entered Vietnam to disarm the Japanese, and that they had been followed by French troops who began the reconquest of Vietnam from the Vietnamese only two months after the war had ended. We learned that the defeat and expulsion of the French from Vietnam was the source of enormous national pride, in the south no less than in the north. These were powerful human forces that we would ignore only at our own peril.

It was well that we began our operations in Vietnam in restricted areas, with scrupulous regard to Vietnamese demands, and with time—no matter how short—to learn to know the people, the environment, and the peculiar circumstances of the war itself. For it was obvious from the beginning that the war would be a strange one.

The United States Marine Corps is trained and equipped as an amphibious assault force of both ground and aviation units. The very nature of this function provides the United States with a force in constant readiness that can go ashore, if necessary, where no port facilities or airfields are available. Neither is it necessary to stockpile supplies ahead of our landing—we bring what we need in the ships that carry us.

There are three other characteristics that are by-products of our amphibious character: the aggressiveness inherent in an elite assault force; the versatility acquired by officers and men who must stand ready to land anywhere, at any time, on short notice; and the high professional quality of a force that must understand ground, naval, and air operations equally in order to fulfill its obligations.

It was this superbly trained and equipped force that we committed as the first American ground combat troops in Vietnam. We had much to learn. The enemy was everywhere and nowhere. He was not uniformed, unidentifiable until he shot at you, unhampered by laws of land warfare recognized by formal states.

The Marines did not enter Vietnam as invaders or as an occupation force. A state of war did not and still does not exist. We found ourselves in Vietnam at the request of its own government—a government so weakened by attack that it retained only vestigial control over its own people and territory.

My own circumstances, as commander of the Marines, were especially peculiar. We Marines were in the I Corps area of the Vietnamese Army. The Vietnamese commander was responsible to his own Army command in Saigon; I was responsible to Gen. William Westmoreland, who commanded all American forces in Vietnam. I was also designated as the American advisor to the Vietnamese commander of I Corps and as the senior officer of the U.S. Naval Services in all of Vietnam. I commanded my own support facilities and also the Marine division within my own force.

Yet my burden was light compared with that of the individual fighting man in Vietnam. When he set foot out of the collective protection of his unit's bivouac area, he entered a world of cloudy danger with both official and personal restraints upon his own actions. The land mine and booby trap were a constant danger. Each hut or hedgerow could, and commonly did, conceal an individual sniper. Each hamlet he approached across the flat green fields could contain an enemy unit. And amid the tension of this constant High Noon atmosphere was the presence of women, children, and old men, presumably, but not always, innocent.

We found an old woman mining a road. We learned that she and a small granddaughter were the only survivors of a family destroyed by war. She did not plant the mines in hate, but only to preserve her granddaughter's life. The Viet Cong brought the mines to her, each time trading the life of the child for her cooperation. This woman was no more an enemy than the mothers of the men she might kill, yet many could die by her hand. It was that kind of war.

In this environment it would have been easy to embitter the population toward us by the use of unnecessary force. We could play into the hands of the enemy by incidents of noncombat casualties, destruction of property, or other acts that could be used to foster resentment toward us together with the government of Vietnam and its armed forces. All of us agreed that alienation of the people had to be avoided at all costs. But it was not easy to accept when the cost had to be borne principally by our own men in the field through restraints imposed on them in a hostile situation.

It was mandatory that we not fire into populated areas unless we received fire from them. The common technique of harassing fire, or the interdiction of roads and trails by long-range fire, had to be exercised with extreme care and limited to known enemy targets, unpopulated areas, and curfew hours when all people were warned to stay in their homes.

Under these rules of engagement we could not land our own forces by helicopter near any dwellings, since we were denied the normal protection of preparatory fires. Close coordination with civil as well as military officials became necessary for all our operations. It became common to warn the people by leaflet or loudspeaker broadcast before entering populated areas. On thousands of patrols each month men had to expose themselves to the possibility of sudden fire from the cover of innocent human beings and their small thatched homes, for the enemy soon perceived our restraint, and used it where he could to his advantage.

I was reminded of my early days as a young officer, learning the fundamentals of my profession from men who had fought Sandino in Nicaragua or Charlemagne in Haiti. The Caribbean campaigns had many lessons applicable to Vietnam forty or fifty years later. I could recall the instruction of veterans of those campaigns and their lessons on tempering the fight with an understanding of the people, compassion toward them, and the exercise of good works, even in the midst of war. These lessons were spelled out in the *U.S. Marine Corps Small Wars Manual* (1940):

In regular warfare, the responsible officers simply strive to attain a method of producing the maximum physical effect with the force at their disposal. In small wars, the goal is to gain decisive results with the least application of force and the consequent minimum loss of life. The end aim is the social, economic, and political development of the people subsequent to the military defeat of the enemy insurgent forces. In small wars, tolerance, sympathy, and kindness should be the keynote of our relationship with the mass of the population.

These seemed new ideas to this generation, with Dachau and Belsen, Hamburg and Coventry, Nagasaki and Hiroshima, Seoul and Pyongyang fresh in the history books. But they accepted them swiftly. A prominent European journalist, J. H. Huizinga, in an article in *The Reporter*, March 9, 1967, could write:

> Few things struck me more in my contacts with U.S. military as well as civilian representatives in Vietnam than the absence of presumption and arrogance. They were quiet Americans indeed, remarkably good-humored and long-suffering even under strong provocation. . . . I marveled at the modest, unassuming tones in which these representatives of a superpower spoke of and to their Vietnamese protégés. Judging by what I saw of them, they rarely throw their weight around and do not adopt the superior airs we Europeans often assumed in colonial days.

He was attesting, and he was not the only one, to the reality of an American code of conduct that, despite occasional and sometimes shocking violations, has held true to this day.

Gradually, from our first enclaves at Phu Bai, Danang, and Chu Lai, we began to understand the people and the enemy.

There were organized units of Viet Cong coursing freely through the vast countryside between the cities and major towns—units up to regimental size, well equipped, experienced, and a thousand or more strong. These forces were sufficiently powerful to compress the Republic's armed forces into municipal garrisons. They supported and were supported by the guerrilla structure—armed civil groups at the community level, exercising day-and-night control over the people.

Parallel to this military and paramilitary structure was a political machine from national to hamlet level—administrators, propagandists, and tax collectors—duplicating the offices of the legitimate government and demanding equal tribute of human and material resources from each small community. To the individual Vietnamese, this was an impossible burden: two gov-

Strange Country, Strange War

ernments, two conscription systems, two collections, two means of reprisal against him for cooperating with the other side. Small wonder the people were impossibly poor in their own rich land. Yet they had endured until we came, and their strength was a solid foundation beneath all the chaos.

The reality that the individual Marine in daily contact with the people saw very quickly, and that all of us came to realize in the first few months, was that these people were neither hostile nor friendly. They were apathetic, stunned by a generation of war, fearing both sides of the military conflict. They were seeking only survival, of the individual, the family, and the small community. They had reason to resent any military force that brought war to their peaceful communities. But we found they were not prepared to hate us unless we gave them reason for it; neither were they prepared to hate their own government or the Viet Cong without similar reason.

It was a new kind of war we were in, where concern for the people was as essential to the battle as guns or ammunition, where restraint was as necessary as food or water. It was a war requiring a stronger discipline than it took to seize Mount Suribachi, and a war filled with new problems, demanding new solutions.

4
New Problems,
New Solutions

Since the surrender of Japan, the Marines had fought in the summer heat of South Korea and in the subarctic cold of North Korea; they had landed against a modern army at Inchon and landed again in Lebanon and the Dominican Republic. Now they were in Southeast Asia.

Although one of the criticisms leveled at military men in general (and generals in particular) is that they always start to fight a war the way the last one ended, none of us expected Vietnam to be much like anything we had experienced before. Initially it was extremely difficult to recognize the true nature of the war and the manner in which it had to be fought. The guerrilla and his infrastructure had a stranglehold on the people. It was a new kind of war, with unique ground rules. We expected problems and knew we would have to find solutions.

Fortunately, it is in the nature of free men to respond creatively to challenge, and we were not disappointed by the breed of Americans we took into Danang, Phu Bai, and Chu Lai. Answers to our problems kept welling up from the men who were doing the fighting. Others came from the foresight of men who years ago had provided us with material and techniques that were particularly applicable to the conflict in Vietnam.

New Problems, New Solutions

To me, as a commander, the helicopter was one of the most significant differences of this war. Since Guadalcanal, as both a battalion and regimental commander in combat, I had chafed at my progressive isolation from the places where the battles were being fought. Modern warfare seemed to doom the commander to sit in some cubicle and fret out each bit of information that came in, hoping it was correct and not missing some small but vital fact.

The helicopter ended this dismal restriction. Like the horse a century earlier, it lifted the commander above the tumult and let him speed from place to place with comparative ease and safety. This new Pegasus allowed me not only to see what was going on, but also to know, first hand, what the men of my command were enduring, and to learn, assess, and pass on to others each unit's response to the circumstances of Vietnam.

As the months went by, many such techniques were refined in practice and put to general use. Some acquired names for convenience; all were passed on to those who succeeded us.

County Fair

The war is among the people, and it is allegiance or control of the people that is at the root of the conflict. It is all-important not to forget the people, as sometimes happens; and to try to see our actions through the eyes of the people. . . .

There had been a soft rain during the night and the smell of the wet fields came into the hamlet on the light breeze that precedes the dawn. The men of the households were still asleep, but the women were up. It was planting time and the days were long. The men would need food in their bellies for the hard work of plowing and harrowing. The shadows of the women shifted on the thatch walls as they added charcoal to still-warm embers, and the flames brightened.

New Problems, New Solutions

The eastern sky was lightening when the morning calm was overwhelmed by an enormously amplified voice using the local dialect: "Do not be afraid, no harm will come to you, but you must follow instructions. Do not leave your homes until we tell you. Do not leave the hamlet until we guide you. You will not be harmed, do not be afraid."

The men awoke with the voice in their ears. In spite of its words they were afraid, and there was fear in their women's eyes and in the eyes of their children, for there is much for a peasant to fear in a world at war, and although each of them was desperately poor, each had something to lose, if only his life. It is one thing to be told that no harm will come; it is another to know that harm is everywhere except among your own family and the people of your own hamlet whose blood is mixed with yours.

So, in spite of the voice, they sat in fear as the day brightened, and they watched in fear the strangeness of it all. What could be seen from the outer huts was quickly passed in whispers through the hamlet:

Americans were all around, with their pale eyes and their hairiness. There were some Vietnamese, too, but soldiers and a few policemen in their blue and white uniforms, not friends or relatives. There was one Vietnamese in civilian dress, and his was the voice, spoken through one of the American machines, that made him sound big as a mountain although he was a smallish man.

The Americans multiplied with a roar and rumble of trucks and began working in their quick way, tents and furniture blossoming like magic; the odor of rich food reminded everyone that the stunning events of the morning had interrupted his own meager breakfast. Some tried to return to normal and prepared the morning meal, but most continued to watch in fascination and dread.

Everyone knew that the brother of Cho had come to his

[34]

house last night with another Viet Cong—a tax collector—to notify each farmer how much he should plant for the use of the Liberation Army at the next harvest. They knew he and his companions were still in Cho's house, and perhaps they would successfully conceal their weapons and behave like any other poor peasants. The inhabitants had no love for the brother of Cho, for he was a strict man, marked with pocks, who knew everyone in the village. It was he who picked the young men of the hamlet to go into the mountains and be soldiers, even though he knew they were needed for work in the fields, and it was he who told the tax collector which farmer was lying when he told how many kilos of rice he could produce each harvest. He was a much feared man, for those who opposed him were also taken into the hills, some never to return, and one had been killed openly by two Liberation soldiers in front of his own house as a lesson to all.

Now they were receiving instructions from the great voice: each family to leave one member in their house, a speaking child or elder if such a one lived there, the rest to leave the hamlet by way of the east path and congregate where the Americans had placed the tents.

The odor of food grew stronger as they approached the tents, trooping out of the hamlet, regretting their missed breakfast. It wasn't until they were assembled that they realized the food was for them. Still fearful of the Americans and their strange ways, they filed past the steaming containers and were pleased to see familiar food—rice and meat in a savory sauce—heaped into bowls in truly surprising quantity. A few sneaked a quick glance at the tax collector and Cho's brother. They noted with relief that both had concealed their rubber-tire sandals as well as their weapons and had smudged their soft hands with dirt and charcoal. Both were hard men, and they did not look frightened in the same way the peasants did, glumly eating their food in a curious, wooden manner.

New Problems, New Solutions

Those who finished first were taken to a nearby tent, and the Vietnamese civilian talked to them, and all the others as they finished, in groups of fifteen or twenty. He was a government official, even more important than the village and district chiefs. He explained how the government was trying to help them, and how the Americans were their friends; how the Viet Cong were trying to destroy all that was good and the government was trying to stop them; how the forces of the government and the Americans were great and strong and had pushed the Viet Cong into the hills.

Only it was also necessary, he explained, to find the small groups who crept in and around the hamlet like the little worms that sometimes get into the sugar cane; and as the farmer cuts out the stalks of cane and burns them when they are infested with the little worms, so must the government now root out these Viet Cong who eat upon the people as the worms eat upon the cane.

Then they were collected together by family and led to another tent, where the police checked each against their own identification records and the cards held by the people. There were many things to explain—births and deaths and relatives who had come from other hamlets and others who had gone to Danang—and it was necessary to lie about the young ones who had been taken away by the Viet Cong, and those like Cho's brother who had joined the National Liberation Front because his face was pocked and he thought the girls detested him for his appearance, although he was strong and would have made a good husband and farmer.

Cho was the spokesman for his family group and said truly that his brother was a member of the family and untruly that he was a simple farmer like the rest. His brother's identification card was correct, but his hands were soft under the dirt and his feet were hard from his traveling, not puckered like the feet of the others who were wading each day now in the warm muck of the paddies, preparing them for planting. Cho and his brother were taken separately to another tent, well surrounded by barbed wire.

The tax collector had attached himself to a different family, and pretended he did not know Cho and his brother. But when he saw them led off, his nerve broke and he tried to run away. He was a quick, nimble man, and there were shouts when he leaped over the encompassing wire, and then rifle fire as he ran for the cover of the bamboo grove that was used as a common source of building material by the villagers. He fell short of the shelter of the grove, half in its shadow, half in the sun, and they left him there for a while, until two Vietnamese soldiers took his body away in a poncho.

As each family was screened through the police tent, they received new identification cards, and new records were made of their names. The busy Americans had put up loudspeakers on poles, and now that instructions over the great voice were no longer needed, there was music, Vietnamese music: "Ai Noi Voi Em," "Moi Lan Trong Boi," and other plaintive songs so popular among the young Vietnamese, as well as some of the older songs and a war march or two. The Americans also provided great tubs of ice-cold drink, sweet to the taste and bright as a pomegranate, and the children drank it until their bellies were as round and tight as melons.

There was another tent where everyone ended up, with pictures that moved and talked as if they were alive, and sweet things to eat, and something for each child from the Americans —a soft cotton shirt, a writing tablet and pencil, a ballpoint pen in the bright red and yellow of the Vietnamese flag—but before anyone could go there he had to pass through a tent where each was looked at by a big American, gentle, but with arms like clubs, and a Vietnamese nurse, pretty in her glistening white *ao-dai*. This tent was filled with medicines and aromatic soap and silver instruments. Many left this tent with soothing salve on sores that had plagued them for days, with eyes or ears cleaner than they had been for weeks, with white gauze bandages on clean and smarting cuts that had previously been open and dirty.

Many adults were also taken aside and talked to quietly by earnest young Vietnamese men or women. They were asked about their problems and their grievances, their aspirations for themselves and for their children. For many this was the first time they had ever thought in such a manner; for almost all it was the first time anyone in authority had displayed an interest in an individual peasant except to draft or tax him. So, many talked freely, and at length—some even talked about the Viet Cong.

Toward the evening meal it was over and the Americans were striking the tents. The people went back to their homes and found that while little had been disturbed, each place had been thoroughly searched. The children and elders who had remained behind said each cave and tunnel had been entered and probed, each urn of rice examined, even the manure piles turned and searched. The weapons of Cho's brother and the tax collector had been found beneath Cho's hearth, and their shoes under the family shrine.

It had been a long day, and there was additional work to do in the morning, with the planting delayed a day, but there was comfort in the full stomachs, and in the happiness of the children with their gifts from the Americans. There was comfort in the soothed cuts and sores, too. Although there was concern at the Vietnamese platoon of young Popular Force soldiers who stayed in the hamlet after everyone else had gone, there was also comfort in the knowledge that someone cared that the hamlet existed at all—for the villagers this was the strangest thing of all in a strange day.

Whether it was the Americans who gave cold drinks or the Vietnamese boy with the glasses who listened to a complaint or the big but gentle man washing out a baby's eyes, the day seemed filled with strangers who cared. The elders were together as the sun lowered into the western mountains, and their talk was low, and the people of the hamlet sensed their questions were the same as in the minds of all the people: Is it true that anyone cares enough to be gentle and kind? Can the powerful give as well as take? Is there such a thing as government that does not only demand? Quietly they pondered the answers.

Such was a County Fair operation, repeated time and again, at first only to find the local guerrillas; later, as the beginning of a long-term pacification effort within a community. As a military tactic it was nothing new—a cordon-and-search operation, in use for centuries. What was new were such things as the explanation offered the people, the food and medical attention provided, shelter from the sun or rain, and decent regard for the community as individuals and families. It was a way in this new kind of war, and it worked well for us.

Rough Rider

The first truck bounced heavily over the abandoned railroad track that crossed the road just outside the village of My Chanh. Behind it was a long column of vehicles that stretched south until it disappeared in the distance.

This was National Route 1, between Hué and Quang Tri, the same infamous road the French called *la rue sans joie*—the Street Without Joy. Now, it was an overland supply route between thousands of Americans and South Vietnamese blocking invasion from the North, and the big supply bases around Hué and Danang. As it had been for the French, the Street Without Joy was vulnerable to many types of attack: mines, snipers, mortar fire, and ambush.

[39]

New Problems, New Solutions

There was only one driver in the first truck, Pfc. Robert L. Franklin of Bellview, West Virginia, United States Marine Corps. Franklin was sitting over two filled sandbags; there were three more at his feet and eight in the empty space beside him. Four sandbags hung from each fender, two were lashed to each running board and the gas tank was shielded by several more. Instead of cargo, Franklin's truck held a hundred and sixty filled sandbags, covering the floor and sides. Beneath his vehicle mechanics had bolted a sheet of quarter-inch steel the length and breadth of the cab and body. Franklin was the "mine finder" for the convoy of trucks that followed him—trained to detect suspicious marks or objects on the road, alert to snipers and ambush, protected to the fullest extent possible from the blast and fragmentation of a mine.

Trucks such as Franklin drove might be completely destroyed by a mine, but the inertia of the sandbags absorbed so much energy from the blast that serious injury to the driver was uncommon. Still, it was a dangerous, lonely, nerveracking task. It is a hundred and ten miles from Danang to Dong Ha, the longest convoy route in Vietnam, and men like Private Franklin drove it almost daily, rolling through the Street Without Joy as part of the day's work.

Behind Franklin's sandbagged vehicle were three dump trucks loaded with dirt, then three more, carrying bridging material. There were extra men in these vehicles: a minesweeping team, two ordnance specialists, and an engineer support team. They could detect and destroy mines, fill in holes blown in the road, and repair or reinforce bridges. After the engineer vehicles came an Army truck, manned by soldiers and armed with four machine guns that could pour out a stream of bullets a half inch in diameter.

Next in line were two jeeps, the convoy commander and his radios, followed by scores of cargo trucks, with every now and then another Army machine-gun truck or one loaded with Marine infantry. The artillery observer was hardly noticeable in the dust and rumble of the column; neither was the young pilot and his radio, ready to talk to the aircraft above. Finally, three wreckers rolled by, bringing up the rear, and the dust settled and it was quiet again. Franklin drove on up the Street Without Joy, his eyes on the road ahead and a hundred trucks behind him.

This time, they made it all the way without an incident—another routine run, unglamorous, undramatic, necessary. Franklin and the other drivers knew it wasn't always so smooth, especially Franklin, in the lead. He knew of the driver in "B" Company whose truck was completely destroyed, engine and cab blown apart by fifty pounds of TNT buried in the road. Miraculously, the driver had picked himself out of the wreckage, bruised a bit and complaining of a ringing in his ears, but otherwise unhurt. Not all were that lucky. There was the one who hit a mine just south of Danang. He was blown upward, then he hit the steering wheel and bounced back down to the seat. The ruptured gas tanks caught fire, and the truck was burned completely. The driver got out alive, but with painful bone separations from the blast.

We called these convoys "Rough Riders," for obvious reasons, and the Viet Cong were never able to stop them. There was much more to them than the column of trucks on the road. We never moved them out unless we had radio contact with them all the way, armed aircraft overhead to cover them, and artillery or naval gunfire on call when they wanted it. Each convoy passed through a series of checkpoints, and its progress was marked at both ends until the destination was reached.

We knew their position within minutes. Combat units were held in readiness to assist any convoy in trouble, but were seldom needed. There was plenty of fight in each convoy, and we soon learned to ignore the occasional sniper round and concentrate on the main issue: moving on. The Viet Cong learned that Rough Riders were tough—tough enough to take on more than they could usually muster. They learned also that stopping a Rough Rider brought artillery or naval shelling, air spotters, and air strikes, turning the hunters into the hunted and the quick into the dead.

So the convoys rolled: for a hundred and fifty miles, up and down the coast, from the base at Chu Lai in the south to Dong Ha near the Demilitarized Zone; along Liberty Road, built by the Marines, from Danang to the An Hoa Civilian Industrial Complex, a thirty-mile lifeline; inland, as far as Khe Sanh, near the Laotian border. Convoys two or three miles long, with millions of dollars' worth of equipment and supplies; hundreds of men commanded by young lieutenants or captains not long out of college. A motor column was ambushed now and then and you read the story in Milwaukee or New York, because there was not much story in the hundreds of convoys that are run each year without incident by men who are too young to have heard of the Street Without Joy and too busy doing their job to care.

The people of Vietnam—and there are millions of them along Route 1 alone—did not need to read the papers. They saw and knew that things were different from before.

We could have depended almost entirely on sealift and airlift between major points on the north-south road through our area, but like many other things in Vietnam, the purely military consideration was never fully adequate. It was important that the roads be kept open for the people as well as for ourselves.

The roads would have been mined whether we used them or not. They were mined when we arrived, and they were indiscriminately mined against civilian and military vehicles alike all the time I was there. Hosts of private vehicles would follow our convoys wherever they went, going from town to town in their wake. The economic and social bloodstream was moving again, and we intended that it continue to flow.

Kit Carson Scouts

The tragedy of war in one's own homeland is not easy for a modern American to visualize. It has been more than a hundred years since armies clashed in the continental United States. Although we still bear some of the scars of that awful conflict, the actual sound of guns is three generations in our past. Today, in Vietnam, the wounds are fresh and newly inflicted each day.

The mystique that has developed over some supposed chasm between East and West seems to me largely nonsense. You can be baffled as easily by the actions of your own brother as by those of someone "East of Suez." These are men and women, and they know joy and sorrow, celebrate new life and mourn their dead as any of us do. It is only in not recognizing that each Vietnamese has lived a life cast in a mold of war and strife that we have difficulty in understanding them.

I have said earlier that a man (or woman) is a Viet Cong for any of several reasons: impressment, protection of the family, adventure, social justice, hero worship, hope for advancement, patriotism, and, rarely, ideology.

They also leave the ranks of the Viet Cong by the thousands each year, again for a variety of reasons: hunger, disease, danger and fear, a dressing-down by some Party functionary, the constant humiliation of "self-examination" before their fellows, or the constant indoctrination lectures; again, rarely for any change in ideology. Quite commonly a man leaves the Viet Cong (or North Vietnamese Army) because he finds he has been deceived; when, in spite of what he has been told, he discovers that the people are against him, that the Americans are not depraved beasts subjugating their country, that he is fighting Vietnamese patriots no different from himself.

The idea of Kit Carson Scouts—former Viet Cong working

[43]

with the Marines—originated with the normal interrogation of former enemy soldiers in detention camps or rehabilitation centers where the Vietnamese government tries to fit them back into the society.

We found many who felt deceived by the Viet Cong; who were furious at their former leaders, and saw peace for their country only if they were exterminated or driven off. Some asked to join with us in doing this—they had much to offer. Most of these were local guerrillas, intimately familiar with a relatively small area, knowing not only every trail and hiding place, but also the names and personalities of the other guerrillas, their tactics and techniques, strengths and weaknesses. They knew our weaknesses, too, as only an enemy can know them.

With the full cooperation of the Vietnamese government, we began to accept some of these volunteers, cautiously at first because of the obvious danger both to the volunteer and to our own men. We waited for one of them to turn against us, or lead a Marine unit into an ambush—it didn't happen. Instead, we found no adequate substitute for their knowledge.

Still with great care we expanded the system, with the goal of providing two Scouts for each rifle company. Each volunteer was investigated and interviewed, then given a period of field trial working with a Marine unit, providing information on the Viet Cong, identifying Viet Cong and their hiding places. One Marine, picked for his genuine interest in the Scouts, was assigned to the Vietnamese volunteer, closely observing him, but also making sure he received proper treatment and was accepted as a member of the unit. Most of the Kit Carson Scouts are young men, around twenty, about the same age as the Marines they work with. In spite of the language barrier there is a quick rapport between them.

When one of these young men passes through the initial period of observation, he is given a complete issue of equipment, is armed, undergoes a short but intensive period of training, and then begins to live and work entirely with the Marine unit. He receives the normal Marine ration, becomes eligible for medical care, is paid at the same time as the Marines, and is allowed three days' leave each month. If he has a family, they are located in a secure area to prevent any reprisal against them by the Viet Cong.

Usually, the Scouts are assigned to a Marine unit in pairs, to share their common language and help overcome the problems of adjustment. There is no way to count the number of American lives saved through the Kit Carson Scouts; we know only that none has been lost through them.

These are former Viet Cong. They have seen both sides of the conflict and have made a choice at great risk to themselves. Their lives, as well as those of our Marines in Vietnam, have been too real and hard to retain illusions—illusions held by those of their own age who, innocent of their meaning, wave the black flag of anarchy or the red flag of revolution in the United States.

Here was one Scout's response to anarchy and revolution— not waved from a campus building, but brought to his country and people by naked, brutal force: Khoan was on patrol with a Marine platoon. Approaching some rice straw stacks, he suspected ambush. It was just such a spot as he would have picked himself a few months earlier. Asking the Marines to stay back a moment, Khoan approached the stacks alone and suddenly fired into them. Before the Marines could close to the area, the lone Scout had fought it out with an entire Viet Cong unit, emptying his own rifle, seizing and firing Viet Cong weapons, bullets tearing at his own body as he fought. It was over quickly. Khoan was wounded in three places. But the ambush was destroyed and the Viet Cong were driven off with heavy losses—the work of one man fighting against an anarchy and revolution he had come to know too well.

New Problems, New Solutions

Here was another's response to the same threat: Thiet was still young, but he had fought for two years with the Viet Cong. He fought against injustice and to end the suffering of the poor people of his country, but he was also a soldier and had to fight as he was told. At first he fought against the government soldiers, mining the roads their trucks used and sometimes hiding in the cemetery near his village to detonate the mines just as the trucks passed over them. Later, Thiet was required to collect taxes from the poor people, and although they did not have enough food for their own families, he had to take rice from them to feed the Liberation Army troops.

Things worsened after the Americans came, and Thiet was required to kill some of the villagers who no longer cooperated with the Viet Cong. One day he had to blow up a schoolhouse so the people would be frightened of the Viet Cong, and this troubled him greatly. Still, he was a soldier and required to do his duty.

One day, Thiet and five others were ambushed by the American Marines as they were leaving a village laden down with confiscated rice. Three of his friends were killed and two wounded and captured, but Thiet was in the rear and escaped to a nearby cave. From there, he watched his two wounded comrades bandaged by the Marines, saw them offered cigarettes and water. Thiet thought of the lectures he had received on how the Americans tortured and killed his people and starved and brutalized the peasants, and he thought on what he and his comrades had been required to do because they were soldiers of the National Liberation Front, of the Vietnamese people they had killed and the rice they had taken from the poor people and the school they had blown up, even though the people wanted it.

There was a hurt deep inside Thiet when he thought of the things he had done, and a rising heat of anger when he remembered the lies he had been told. Now, before him, the very men depicted as the most inhuman and brutal had performed the first kind act he had seen in many months. His hands above his head, Thiet walked out into the sun toward the little group of men.

Several months later Thiet, Kit Carson Scout, approached the same cave. He was no longer a soldier. Thiet believed the best thing for his people was for the Viet Cong to lay down their arms and help build a new country in peace. He was a Kit Carson Scout for only one reason: to tell his former comrades to kill no more and be killed no more. The Marines understood this and did not use him in any other way. Through Thiet nineteen Viet Cong had already surrendered.

Now, as they approached the cave he knew so well, he saw five men he immediately recognized as Viet Cong darting into the concealed entrance. Without fear Thiet went into the cave alone, and there, in the dark, he talked with them. The Marines, waiting some distance away, saw four men come out, their hands in the air. A fifth man, starting out behind the others, hesitated and went back into the cave. There was a muffled explosion and a puff of grayish smoke from the cave mouth.

Thiet had told people, "I think I will be killed some day, but before I am, perhaps I can do some things to help my country become a place where the people do not live in fear." No one will ever know what happened in the cave; whether an old friend took another's life with his own, in hate and retribution, or whether two old friends, saddened at the betrayal of their youth, no longer cared to live.

Two nations honored Thiet at his burial: his own and ours. For Thiet died a wise man and a man of good will, worthy of honor. He had fought against injustice with the Viet Cong; he had fought against tyranny with the United States Marine Corps; and, however he died, he died a patriot.

Stingray

The little team made its terse and laconic report over the radio: group of twelve adult males, ten armed with rifles or submachine guns, two carrying heavy packs, sighted at a certain time and place, moving east; called in artillery; results: one known survivor, fleeing west.

The voice came quietly through the speaker. Its owner and four other Marines were atop a mountain deep inland. They had been there almost a week, taking turns in a tree perch, watching the trails, ridgelines, and valleys for enemy movement. They lived like jungle cats, silent and cautious and deadly—for long-range artillery and swift jet aircraft were ready to strike at their request, suddenly and with great power, guided by those hidden eyes in the bush. This was Stingray.

The Stingray concept developed from a unique organization in the Marine division: the reconnaissance battalion. These men are the eyes and ears of the commander, dozens of small teams operating night and day for no other purpose than information. We found, in Vietnam, that much of the vast amount of information fed to us by these teams referred to fleeting targets, small groups of armed men, identifiable as Viet Cong by their location, in constant movement to and from the inland mountains.

So, Stingray was formed—not so called at first, but operating as forward observers for artillery or naval gunfire as well as observation posts; later, after some special training, acting also as forward air controllers, directing air strikes against targets too large or too remote for effective use of artillery. This was dangerous work, but done by experts, inflicting enormous casualties on the Viet Cong in areas they had previously called their own, without taking any significant casualties ourselves.

The endurance, patience, and skill of these men were—and

remain—phenomenal. Their patrols were measured in hours, not days or nights, for deep in enemy territory every moment is a threat and there is neither true rest nor relief from constant vigilance. The men came off those patrols with a peculiar, haunted look. Veterans of this type of work had in common a dangerous expression that was never quite lost, even after long rest, and that was accentuated by their leanness.

Consider one patrol: a hundred and ninety-three hours out, thirty-two separate sightings, thirty-two calls for artillery fire or air strikes. The patrol was never detected by the enemy, sustained no casualties.

Consider another: three hundred and eighty-eight hours out, sixty-four sightings, called for artillery sixty times, for air strikes twice; not one American casualty.

And consider two hundred or more of these patrols each month, not all equally successful, but each contributing to a massive coverage of every likely enemy movement, a constant chipping-away at his strength, and occasionally an opportunity to find a major force, slipping in from the mountains, bent on destruction, and catch them before they are out of their own hills.

The particular advantage of Stingray was its severe toll on the enemy with no significant loss of our own men. The Marines of the reconnaissance units came to know the hills and valleys of their areas as well as the Viet Cong themselves, and the weapons they used struck with stunning suddenness. The size of the opposing forces meant nothing: a Stingray patrol could take on a thousand men as long as their own location remained a secret.

Jerry E. Siler was a second lieutenant, but not in the popular image of one. Lieutenant Siler had enlisted in the Marine Corps from Omaha, Nebraska, had fought in Korea, where he received the Silver Star for heroism, and worked his way up through the ranks to a commission.

New Problems, New Solutions

In December of 1966 he took a patrol into the foothills west of Hué. The weather was cold for Vietnam, foggy and rainy; their area was covered with scrub brush, waist to shoulder high. Patrolling each day, holing up at night, they encountered increasing numbers of Viet Cong. There was one clash with a group of about fifteen, a Marine wounded and evacuated by helicopter. Afterward the Viet Cong became bolder, as if they believed the patrol had been pulled out with the wounded man. Patiently, Siler and his men lay low and listened to their enemy laugh, joke, and talk loudly.

After one more wet, cold night they moved to a small hill from which they could observe a valley and trail that seemed to be the focal point of Viet Cong activity. Through the fog and rain, they could see a column of Viet Cong along the trail, in groups of forty or fifty, some carrying mortars, some carrying heavy machine guns—a Viet Cong regiment on the move toward Hué—though the New Year truce of January 1967 had begun that day.

Siler radioed back his information and waited. The terms of the truce permitted firing only when an enemy force appeared to be moving to attack—and a thousand Viet Cong were moving toward Hué with mortars and machine guns.

I received the news personally and called Saigon personally. I believed this to be a legal target under the terms of the truce; that a large enemy force was moving to attack Hué, either during the truce or after they had positioned themselves under its cover. Saigon agreed, and I was told to shoot.

All available guns were laid on the target; all Marine aircraft capable of bad-weather operations were standing by. We told Siler to move out. He and his fourteen men got out as quickly as they could, and moved as far as they could for a half hour. It was almost dark, the Viet Cong column had slowed down in the dusk and rain, when the shells began to fall. For forty-five minutes the area was pounded with everything we had. Siler and his men were still too close for comfort. As the first shells landed they took cover in a stream and stayed there, neck deep in the water, through the artillery barrage and the air strikes that followed.

It rained harder that night and harder again the following day—rained as it can only in the wet monsoon of Southeast Asia. We sent in a rifle company to cover Siler and his patrol, still skirting groups of three to ten Viet Cong in the area, and got them out safely. What happened to the Viet Cong column we can merely surmise. But we do know that Hué was not attacked that month.

This was the type of incident that decimated the Viet Cong on pathways and in unpopulated areas they had called their own for a decade or more. Stingray took men with a high degree of skill and a lot of nerve. We had them, and they were worth many battalions to all of us.

Golden Fleece

The villagers of Hoa Vang District were troubled. For years the Viet Cong had circulated before each harvest and assessed a tax in paddy—threshed but unmilled rice—based upon the amount of standing grain. Sometimes they were lenient and asked for only a quarter of the harvest; sometimes they were severe and demanded up to 90 per cent of the farmer's crop. But always they had come during harvest time, and the peasants were made to carry the product of their own labor into the hills to the secret caches of the Viet Cong.

This year it was different. The American Marines had come, and such was their strength in Hoa Vang District that although the Viet Cong could still assess the tax, they were unable to get it back into the hills. So they had sent the word: "Do not harvest your rice this year; let it rot in the fields. If you do not do as we say, we will attack your villages and you will die and your homes will be burned." This was the sadness of the people of Hoa Vang District, for they would be beggared or would starve if they could not have even a part of the grain now fat in their fields and ripening for harvest.

The commander of the Marine battalion that guarded Hoa Vang District heard of the villagers' plight and made a plan. He would cover the area with guards and patrols, keeping mobile forces in reserve, all through the harvest. He would work with the district chief to provide safe storage for the harvested grain, and work out a system of credit by which each family could draw their rice as they needed, to eat or to sell. He called his plan "Golden Fleece."

The common Vietnamese method of storing threshed rice is in big ceramic urns, each holding perhaps two bushels. At the end of the first Golden Fleece operation more than seventeen thousand urns stood in safe storage. It had been years since the farmers had realized the full benefit of their hard labor, and the people were happy.

During the harvest the Viet Cong tried to make good their threat, first with patrols, then with larger units, finally with a battalion. Each time they were beaten back. Unsuccessful in their attempt at overt attack, the Viet Cong began infiltrating into the harvest area by individuals. These tried to get rice out by boat to Viet Cong areas and to mine the paddies so harvesters would be killed in their own fields. River patrols and ambushes were set up to counter this attempt, and Marine engineers checked the paddies for mines before they were harvested.

Patrols were sent into the nearby hills to locate and if possible return rice already confiscated and hidden by the Viet Cong. The results validated the villagers' complaints of heavy taxation. Tons of hastily hidden rice were found around the area, two tons here, three tons there, a nest of old gasoline drums filled with freshly harvested rice, a heap of loose rice estimated at three hundred bushels dumped into an open roofed shelter in the hills.

As the fields bared, the activity subsided in Hoa Vang District, but we saw with new eyes the progress of the harvest throughout the huge area of our responsibility.

There were two harvests a year. February and September in the north around Hué; May and October in the Danang area. This was immutable, and we could plan ahead each year to deny as much rice as possible to the Viet Cong and retain as much as possible in the hands of the farmers or available to them on demand. (Large land holdings, absentee ownership, and tenant farmers were never a problem in the I Corps area. Almost all the farmers were tilling family lands owned by actual title or by ancient custom.) The rice production of the land would be denied the Viet Cong, and the peasant and his family would not see the fruits of their labor carried off into the hills.

It would have been impossible not to have expanded Golden Fleece operations. The peasants asked for it. After the example at Hoa Vang each Marine unit at harvest time was approached by the local people with the same request: save our rice too.

The government of Vietnam responded with means for inventory and control, with local guard forces and communal transportation from the fields to safe storage. Sometimes the villagers who feared Viet Cong confiscation put their urns of rice into the hands of friends or relatives in safer areas, sometimes they brought them to the government warehouses. The Agency for International Development provided cement and tin for the construction of dry buildings in safe areas, and the people filled them with rice urns.

The Viet Cong tried to fight the system, but they were no longer the fish swimming in a sea of cooperative people: they were sharks, attacking the peasants as they worked. In areas still controlled by the Viet Cong the rice tax soared and its enforcement became harsher. The people in these areas became more than ever disaffected with the Viet Cong, and they fought back in the only ways they could—hiding their rice or moving into government areas as refugees, leaving their ancestral fields untilled. Each catty of rice—the pound-and-a-third measure used in the Orient—not going into Viet Cong bins meant that another catty had to be grown in North Vietnam and brought over the hundreds of miles of mountain trail by human bearers. We were winning another segment of the struggle in the rice paddies.

There were many other problems and other solutions, each greater than itself alone, cumulative in effect at each gain or loss. The net result was progress in the battle against the armed enemy, in bettering the lot of the people, in solidifying and strengthening the legitimate government. I used to tell my staff and subordinate commanders, "I need more than your loyalty and effort. I need your ideas." They did not disappoint me.

5

Chevron
War

A corporal and eleven men. One patrol of hundreds on a hot
July day—keeping the Viet Cong holed up, disrupting their
movements, chipping at their strength with every chance encounter; a never-ending job, night and day, with corporals and
sergeants bearing the burden of command and the responsibility of decision.

They had gone a long way by the time they reached the
stream. Canteens were low, and they needed a short rest, so
Cpl. Laurence J. Brent gave the silent hand signals to halt and
disperse to cover.

These were seasoned men who faced outward automatically
and kept watch without command. Brent picked three to collect canteens and fill them at the stream under watchful protection of the rest. No one had seen a movement. No one had
heard anything but the careful movements of those at the
water when the hot, still day was slashed by a staccato of small
arms fire. A force of more than fifty Viet Cong had opened fire
on the water detail. Corporal Brent was about to earn his pay.

Immediately he directed covering fire. The three men with
the canteens dove into concealment and wormed their way
back to the patrol, dashing the last few yards and turning,

winded, into position to add their fire to the fight. The enemy shifted, and Brent could tell from the sound of their weapons that some had come around to his left and others were moving farther on to his rear. He faced this new threat with his machine gun, using it as cover to pull back onto a slight rise of ground. This meant getting up, where his men—and the Viet Cong—could see him, and leapfrogging his patrol back to the rise, a team at a time, moving fast under fire, bent almost double, while the others tried to fire faster.

In such a situation the body responds with almost superhuman qualities. Vision becomes panoramic, the mind acts with such clarity and speed that events seem to occur in slow motion.

Somehow, in all he was doing, with the Viet Cong fire cracking and ringing about him, Brent saw two helicopters approaching, drawn to the fight by its flash and dust. Quickly, as they came on, he identified the situation to them with colored smoke grenades—red smoke tossed at the enemy, green smoke in and about his own position.

By this time the Viet Cong had brought a mortar into play and began to shell the area, but their nerve broke under the fire from the helicopters and they flushed from their positions. Brent had his men pour fire into them as they scattered—two, eight, twenty, thirty down as they broke. Fire low, fire fast; empty the magazine and reload; count your ammo; twenty here, twenty there—almost out. There's a day's work with little left for any more. Count your men, Corporal Brent—Jenkins here, Cohen here, all here, none dead, none wounded; down the far side of the hill to the choppers, barely touching the ground with their wheels as you tumble in, off and away. Corporal Brent and eleven out; Corporal Brent and eleven in; another patrol tomorrow. (Corporal Brent, of Chicago, for this and a number of other reasons, is now Lieutenant Brent.)

Chevron War

The night was dark and they moved silently—four men, a Marine fire team, the smallest organized element in the Marine Corps. Their leader, Cpl. Mark E. De Planche of Flint, Michigan, had been given his mission: move outside the company lines several hundred meters to that spot where the stream crosses the trail, set up an ambush—and wait.

Raising his hand, De Planche halted the column. Listen—on the other side of the hill there—sounds like digging; better check it out. The men moved away from the path they had been following and around the base of the hill. Halting again as they reached a clearing, peering into the darkness, scanning the field slowly—back and forth, trying to catch the hint of movement with the sensitive side vision. They are there, but how many and what are they doing? De Planche moved his men forward, creeping on all fours now in the low brush. As he watched a flare from a friendly mortar burst overhead and he could see them: thirty or forty men in a long skirmish line moving toward him, some carrying mortars.

De Planche's mind raced. What should he do? He could steal back around the base of the hill with his men, make a report by radio, and bring in artillery fire on the Viet Cong. But would there be time? The alternative was for his fire team to take on a guerrilla band ten times its number. The decision had to be made by De Planche—now. The enemy has paused and is setting up his mortars. His gun crews are moving into position; one man picks up a mortar shell—hefting it as if momentarily to drop it down the tube and begin the attack.

A half hour later reinforcements from the Marine company arrived, dispatched when the platoon commander heard the noise of the fight and, minutes later, received a radio report from the fire team. De Planche and his three men had attacked—four rebel yells piercing the stillness of the night, four rifles cracking. A Marine fire team alone had forced forty VC to flee in panic, leaving behind their four mortars, a pile of ammunition, fifteen of their rifles, and four of their dead. Only a fire team lead by a corporal, twenty years old. Uneven odds, a decision made, a battle won.

Such is the chevron war—the war in the hands and minds of young men in their teens and early twenties. Not for almost a hundred years has the American noncommissioned officer borne such a large share of responsibility or such a weight of individual decision. The issue of battle and the lives of his men are dependent on his action alone.

It was that way once before with the Army in the western United States, a hundred years ago: Sergeant Austin at Wounded Knee, Private First Class Barnes at Fort Apache, Corporal Comfort at Staked Plains, Sergeant Denny in Las Animas Canyon, and on through the alphabet to men named Yount and Zeigner. From Arizona in 1861 to Minnesota in 1898, over the span of a whole generation, a war of detachments and patrols led by men with chevrons on their arms.

Such a war had come again. Some of the names were different from before and some were the same, but the incidents and the men were strangely alike except for date, and it didn't even seem surprising when the United States Cavalry came to the rescue—only now they were riding helicopters.

The young Marines with two or more chevrons were as well trained and equipped as we could make them. Helicopters with rockets and machine guns on them could hover overhead. Artillery or mortars could cover every foot of ground on which they stepped. Multimillion-dollar aircraft could be aloft or standing by on the airstrips, ready to take off and deliver five thousand pounds of ordnance at their call. Their officers could worry about them. All of these things could be; but in the final analysis they were alone: it was their decision that counted—this was their war.

Most of the time the work is tense and tedious, without contact with the enemy. You move silently, fearful of making any

Chevron War

sound that might betray your presence. A sudden movement of a bird or jungle animal sets your pulse racing. You freeze, staring hard, trying to see through the maze of vines and bamboo and broad leaves, afraid to blink your eyes for fear of missing that one movement that might mean your life. A minute, three minutes, five minutes pass, and your muscles cramp and your eyes burn. No sound, no movement; take a chance and move on, motion your men forward. All quiet—no contact.

You continue, silently, cursing the packstraps that cut into your shoulders. A blade of "elephant" grass rasps across your hand, leaving a small cut you'll treat as best you can, but it will become infected from that limitless compost pile called the jungle despite your efforts.

Time for a break. Silently motion to your men to spread out —take ten. Don't relax your mind, though. Keep scanning the jungle, keep listening. Can you take a chance on a cigarette? Will the smoke give you away? Roll up your trouser leg—two leeches just above the boot. Put a drop of insect repellent on each: it burns them and they fall off, writhing. You're hungry. Open a can and spoon it down cold. Wash it down with water that tastes bitter from the iodine tablets you put in to purify it. Bury the can—leave no evidence that you were here.

Time to go; still a lot of ground to cover before nightfall. On your feet and move out, wondering if the next instant will bring this eerie, silent world to an abrupt end with the tumult of a two-sided firefight, swift movement, voice commands, open radio communications, and all the shock of infantry battle.

Sometimes the action you anticipate comes not from the Viet Cong but as it happened to Sgt. Richard P. Golden of Norfolk, New York. Leading his patrol deep into the jungle, the sergeant paused at night for a few hours' rest. With half of his men he slept, while the others kept watch until part of the night was gone and it would be their turn to sleep.

Chevron War

Suddenly he awoke in terror as he felt himself being dragged from the perimeter—his shoulder tightly clamped between the jaws of a tiger. His patrol members heard his cries and came to the spot, but were afraid to fire for fear of hitting him. Finally the tiger dragged him into a bomb crater and, loosing his grip, turned to snarl at his pursuers. Sensing their opportunity, they fired and the tiger fell dead. Golden stood up and walked out of the crater.

This is the way it is, though—hours of tension, boredom, and discomfort broken by moments of the rage and fear and pain and triumph and defeat of combat.

The Marines called it "Happy Valley," with the inverse humor of the foot soldier, because it was dangerous even to approach it. Happy Valley was surrounded by jungled mountains covered by the vast triple canopy of the tropics; thick on the bottom with fern and vine, spread halfway up with broadleaf, and covered on the top by giant hardwood a hundred feet or more from the ground spreading over all. The valley floor was a mass of natural bamboo, tough and impenetrable except for hour after painful hour of patient chopping.

Through the mass, both in the highland and on the valley floor, the Viet Minh and their successors, the Viet Cong, had developed a system of trails. Based on the stream beds and the thinner forest at the crest of each ridge, but connected with lateral trails cleared by enormous human labor, the trails led to supply caches, rest camps, training camps, and work areas where impressed labor from the lowlands made uniforms, rubber-tire sandals, explosive mines, and other ordnance.

Lance Cpl. Ralph Bobian of Denver, Colorado, was a machine gunner—a breed unto themselves. A machine gunner feels that he is destined to carry too heavy a load too far; that it is demanded that he keep up with lighter-loaded infantrymen no matter how steep the hill or how deep in mud the flat. Too

Chevron War

often the fight that comes is never long enough to bring to play the weapon he has borne with such labor, but that weapon is always cleaner than any other and seldom wielded by a man with less than phenomenal courage.

So one day Bobian and eight other men went into Happy Valley in the weird midday twilight of the jungle, and they met a Viet Cong unit, nose to nose, as it happens on the narrow, choked trails. Bobian came into play with his machine gun that day, and the power of it put the Viet Cong into panic and confusion. Recovering, they doubled back on the small patrol, and Bobian was ready again, firing from the hip in long, arcing bursts, pushing in on them, until he encountered a Marine wounded in the melee. Bobian covered him with his own body and the fire from his weapon. Hit, he moved forward, propped himself against a bush, and continued to fire long bursts into the green brush, again and again, until he died there, under their fire. One chevron, with crossed rifles below it; lance corporal, United States Marine Corps; Vietnam; five days before Christmas, 1967.

Sgt. Antonio Rangel, San Antonio, Texas: one year in Vietnam; a hundred and twenty-seven patrols; wounded three times. The first, an exploding mine that blew fragments into his arm and leg; the second as he led his men across a paddy against Viet Cong fire; the third a bullet in the leg as he closed with a Viet Cong unit toward the coast. Each time ignoring his wounds until the job was done, refusing evacuation until all his men were cared for; after each wound ready to go again. When it was done, a hundred and twenty-seven times out in the strange and terrible country and there were four scars where bullets or shell fragments had scored his flesh, Sergeant Rangel asked to stay another half year, where the action was, where he had led men on the cutting edge of battle, where his cunning and skill and courage were needed.

Chevron War

Sometimes it calls for a different kind of courage, a different kind of discipline and control. One young Marine—young enough to be a high-school senior—experienced such a moment. As he placed his foot carefully on the trail in front of him, he heard a sharp, metallic *click*. Sensing immediately that he had stepped on a mine, he waited breathlessly for the blast that he knew would blow his foot or leg off at any second. Somehow he kept his head and stood very still, at the same time calling a warning to the other members of his squad to clear the area. A minute that seemed like an hour passed, and he realized that maybe—as long as he kept his foot in place—he was safe. What would happen, though, if he moved his foot? Would the mine go off or was it a dud?

With cold sweat running down his face, he tried to decide what to do. Two of his men started to move to his position, but he ordered them back. Finally, despite his orders, another Marine—an engineer who had almost completed his tour and would be going home in twenty-six days—moved to his side and began probing the ground around his foot. Carefully, he removed the dirt from the deadliest type of mine our men have encountered, a "Bouncing Betty." When activated, this mine hops into the air waist-high and explodes, sending its lethal fragments in all directions.

The engineer continued to dig, carefully removing the dirt until he found the firing device. Looking closely, he saw that the device had been activated, but that the firing pin had failed to strike the detonator. The slightest movement or jar, he realized, could cause it to move the remaining fraction of an inch and detonate the mine.

For twenty-eight minutes, while his squad leader stood motionless and the remainder of the squad held their breath, he worked around the mine. Finally he was able to fashion a makeshift safety pin from a wire, and inserted it in the firing device. He then called each member of the squad forward, one at a time, and they piled their flak jackets around the squad leader's foot. When the last one was in place, the engineer moved back. Would the pin hold? Taking a deep breath, the squad leader jumped. For a split second, while in mid-air, he expected the mine to spring up, spraying fragments into his body. Then it was over, the makeshift safety pin had done the trick, and his left foot had never felt better.

Mines are particularly suited to the guerrilla and the terrorist, and the Viet Cong are clever with them. Again, it is usually the noncommissioned officer and his men who face them directly, bear the casualties from them, and provide the human skill and courage required to reduce their harm. There are many kinds of mines. Most of them are small, but some of them are big enough to sink a ship or fell a bridge.

It was a broad river and a respectable bridge, and the Viet Cong had mined it cleverly. There were two charges, each a hundred-and-twenty-five pounds of explosive. They were fixed to floats that fell with the tide, and the detonators were wired to the bridge. As the tide went out, the floats would drop and the wires tauten until they blew the mines.

This ingenious rig was found by an alert patrol. Cpl. John J. Pontius of Thompsontown, Pennsylvania, was the nearest engineer. The problem was one for a demolition specialist, but Pontius saw that the wires were tightening and time and tide were running fast.

Carefully he cut the first wire and saw its charge towed to the river bank. The ebbing tide had tightened the second wire even more when he went back on the bridge alone. With a hundred-and-twenty-five pounds of explosive dangling below him, ready to go off on the next trough of river current or the next immeasurable slack of tide, Corporal Pontius cut the second wire and defused the attached mine. Two chevrons, two mines, and on to the next job, whatever it might be.

The demands of responsibility, courage, and decision are not confined to the ground troops.

Sgt. Rawlin C. Gull of Tooele, Utah, was crew chief on a Marine helicopter, at his station in the cabin, connected to the pilot above by the umbilicus of a communication cord. Their mission that soggy January day was typical of the fighting in Vietnam: the Marine helicopter was supporting a unit of the Army of the Republic of Vietnam, covered by a heavily armed U.S. Army helicopter. There was a stiff fight going on below in a morass of flooded paddyland.

It happened quickly, as it always does in the air: the Army helicopter was hit and pancaked into the paddies in a geyser of spray and mud, Viet Cong on three sides, and no friendly troops near.

The Marine pilot called for covering fire from another passing helicopter and bored into the fight, his own machine gunner spraying the ground around the crippled machine. He flared his helicopter into a landing nearby, and Sergeant Gull piled out, waist-deep in muck, to aid the Army crew. One was already wounded, no one knew how badly. As the others struggled toward the Marine aircraft, Sergeant Gull got to the wounded man, hoisted him up, floundered through the mud and water and angry whine of Viet Cong bullets, and pushed him into the waiting hands of men already aboard. Quickly giving a thumbs-up signal to the watching—and anxious—pilot, he grabbed the handhold himself as the helicopter lifted off to safety.

At the surge of the machine into the air Sergeant Gull's slime-covered hands slipped off, and he plummeted back into the mud still ruffled and blown by the downdraft of the big rotor blades. For one moment death or years in a prison camp hovered over Sergeant Gull like the big green helicopter above him. Then the pilot, who had felt what had happened by the sudden loss of weight as he lifted off, settled the craft back down to the flooded ground and took on his muddy crew chief. As they took off the second time Sergeant Gull was already back at his station, spraying bullets out of the starboard side to keep the Viet Cong down.

There is no "front" in Vietnam. Wherever you are, whatever your job, the war can be brought to you with shocking suddenness. The Marines have adhered to the principle that every officer and man is trained and equipped to fight as an individual. Three young Marines had occasion to prove it one night.

Cpl. Eugene Mortimer of Las Vegas, New Mexico, and Cpl. Leonard O'Shannon of Portland, Oregon, were aviation electricians; Cpl. Lawrence Brule of Rochester, New York, was an aircraft mechanic. Although none of them thought they would have occasion to use it, each was armed with a rifle and had been trained for individual combat.

It was near midnight, and these three were turning in at the end of a long day of work at the Danang airbase. In quick succession three explosions racked the air. Shoeless and partially dressed, the three Marines grabbed their rifles and dove for the sandbagged hole they had built for protection and, if necessary, for fighting. They hadn't been in position half a minute when O'Shannon saw a group of armed men running toward them.

Two electricians and a mechanic in a hole, with a Viet Cong suicide squad bearing down on the aircraft nearby—submachine guns ready, hand grenades, a rocket launcher, satchels of high explosive to blast the flight line, the fuel dumps, the ammunition magazines.

Thirty feet away. They look like Viet Cong. At least eight of them, probably more there in the night. Coming fast. What do you do?

Fifteen feet away. No command, no headquarters, no information, three corporals in a hole and a decision to be made.

Ten seconds later the heat was radiating from three rifle barrels and the last echo was bouncing off a distant wall. Eleven Viet Cong sprawled around the fighting hole among their satchel charges and grenades, two still moving feebly, the rest motionless.

There are countless examples of fortitude and courage and skill, more than one for each man: daring rescues by helicopter, nerve-racking ambushes in the dark and wet, assaults against hills and into caves, booby traps and land mines, the tense passage of silent, hostile hamlets, or men stalking each other in the thick green gloom of deep forest. The names stand out and I wish I could tell about them all—all the others who fought the chevron war.

These were what we once called the Beat Generation, these are the Hippies and Yippies of today, with only minor differences such as training and conditioning, discipline, and a cause. Bigger and smarter than their fathers or uncles, the men I saw and commanded with such affection and respect are as good as any I have seen in a lifetime of soldiering, and their task is in many ways more difficult. It is not dramatic, rarely witnessed by others, seldom filmed or reported. It is close, vicious, and protracted fighting, largely at night, in small units, with the loneliness of command assumed by young men of high school or college age.

In the fullest measure they have proved their worth. We can be proud of them.

6
Steel
Gauntlet

The bits of information came from various sources—a static-blurred radio message; a whisper in a village; a malaria-ridden prisoner. As each confirmed the other the picture built up like some great jigsaw puzzle and we began to see the basic outline: there was a Viet Cong regiment, assembled and poised to strike at the new airbase being built at Chu Lai.

These were not the local guerrillas, but an organized Main Force unit. Its men were picked from the guerrilla bands after they had demonstrated the necessary courage, dedication, and skill. Although they still wore the black pajamas of the Vietnamese peasant as a uniform, their weapons and equipment were modern and well suited to their method of fighting: many submachine guns, mortars, light and heavy machine guns, recoilless antitank guns, stout and serviceable radio and telephone equipment.

Their plan—what we knew of it—was a good one. They had selected the Marines as a target, to show the people that these impressive-looking foreigners were no match for the Main Force Viet Cong. They had selected Chu Lai as their target since it was the most remote from other American or South Vietnamese forces and offered the chance of annihilating an

[67]

American unit before help could be pushed through mined and blocked highways. These tactics had worked time and again against the Republic of Vietnam. There was no reason at the time they would not work equally well against us—except that they, as well as we, had much to learn.

To confirm the reports, we drifted aircraft across the suspected area, following the usual pattern of flights, but photographing as they passed over. The prints were revealing. They showed a development of field fortifications—zigzag trenches, foxholes, and dugouts—facing inland, their backs to the sea. Encompassed within this ring of breastworks was a quiet little peninsula and several white sand beaches, places where sampans carrying men and supplies could be landed inconspicuously among the hundreds of fishing craft that used the offshore waters. The whole picture was one of a bastion against attack from the mainland, the peninsula its rear area and the sea its road and supply route. The Viet Cong were still fighting last year's war.

First, they were wrongly assuming that the Americans could react no more quickly or could come no nearer to pushing them into the sea than the French or the Republic of Vietnam.

Second, they did not know an assault against them from the sea was not only a possibility, but a specialty as well of the force opposing them.

Finally, their dispositions seemed to give no consideration to the Marines' ability to move by helicopter anywhere they wished, without dependence on overland communications.

Then, the wheel of fortune spun, and several other factors turned up in our favor. Part of a fresh regiment of Marines had just landed at Chu Lai, so recently that they were still unloading when the time for decision came. Along with their sea movement was the normal complement of Navy ships that provided a powerful addition to artillery already ashore. Another Marine battalion was afloat offshore, available as a Special

Landing Force. And, as an almost unbelievable bonus, a Navy cruiser was in the area, ready to support anything we wished to do within the range of her six-inch guns.

What would have happened if we had let the Viet Cong go ahead with their plan we shall never know. Instead, we forced them to battle. Here were two thousand men or more, the main strength of the Viet Cong for several provinces, flushed with victories over the South Vietnamese and ready to prove themselves against us—as well as to prove our inadequacy for their kind of war. It was no time to await their blow.

In addition, there was something special here. Partly by chance and partly by design, the components of a Navy-Marine Corps striking force were on the scene. There was more to this than just guns. We were used to working together under the common military doctrine. We did not have to spell everything out for each other. Teamwork was built in. Our own doctors, dentists, chaplains, and medical corpsmen were Navy. The cruiser offshore had a Marine detachment aboard. The amphibious ships had Marine officers and men as essential components of their staffs and crews. This was the team that had fought through the Pacific and stormed the harbor at Inchon. Only the faces had changed.

Quickly we made our decision.

We would land a battalion of Marines by helicopter well inland, to trap the Viet Cong against the sea. We would use the Navy ships still at Chu Lai—those that had just unloaded the newly arrived units—to reembark another battalion and land it at dawn over the beach in Marine amphibian tractors and Navy landing craft. A third Marine battalion, a Special Landing Force already afloat and cruising offshore for just such an opportunity, would be ready to land by either boat or helicopter when needed.

This was not to be an antiguerrilla war, pacification, revolutionary warfare, or any other aspect of a War of National Liberation. This was a clash of conventional armed forces against conventional armed forces, and it differed only in minor respects from what we had known in World War II and Korea.

My own takeoff time from Danang on the morning of the assault was well before dawn. As we flew south by helicopter little spots of light appeared in the countryside below—the women of Vietnam awaking for a new day and lighting fires for the morning tea and gruel. From our position far above it seemed as if each home had a heart that glowed to strength again after the long night, some still weak, but others already strong and bright.

Gradually, as we went south, the sky lightened over the South China Sea. The dawn does not come up like thunder off Vietnam; it comes gently. When it became light enough, I could see the tortured little spot where the Marines were to land, the hills puffed with smoke, the dirty scud drifting out into the cool bright sea. As we approached the area we dropped our altitude. The last few miles we skimmed just over the water, converging on the landing beach with the first few waves of amphibious craft.

As we landed, the rotor blades of the helicopter humming to a stop, a mine exploded off to the left and there was a crackle of gunfire far to the right. The rest of the area was eerily quiet.

The beach was a good one: firm sand, shelving rather steeply into the sea, with hardly a hint of surf. There was a small village immediately inland. We had thought it might be fortified, but the "rules of engagement" denied any shelling or bombing of inhabited areas. Even if such restrictions had not existed, I would have taken our chances on a slow movement through it rather than senselessly to inflict damage on a possibly peaceful people.

The two rocky promontories to the north and south of the village, however, were under no such restriction, and represented more of a military threat to our landing than the village in the cove. Machine gun or cannon fire raking across the beach from either side of our landing was something I had experienced twenty years ago, and I had no desire to see it repeated on the present generation. The Navy moved in on these targets at first light, and our landing was accompanied with the crash of five- and six-inch shells to either side.

This would have been enough to frighten the villagers away, unless they were held there as hostages for protection of the Viet Cong. When we entered it, we found a simple fishing hamlet, the sampans pulled up on the beach for the night, the fishing nets spread to dry. The sails had been plaited of straw by the women; the anchors had been fashioned of wood by the men and weighted with rocks so they would sink.

The homes of the fishermen were small and neat and quite clean, with thatched roofs and sides of rice-straw matting. They were nicely arranged, with a palm tree here and there for shade and borders of cactus between plots, an occasional cornerpost carved for decoration, and the reverent little shrines in each household. All the people were gone. I saw a big black dog ahead of our Marines as they searched through the village, and an Asian turkey stalking its way into a clump of bamboo, with no other signs of life but the big Marines, looking like Gullivers in Lilliput against the small doors and windows of the Vietnamese houses.

One hut, on the far edge of the village, was burning brightly when we landed. We found later that it had been the Viet Cong headquarters; they had been sufficiently surprised at the dawn landing to have to burn their equipment and flee inland.

Inland of the village was a cultivated area where the fishermen and their families grew staples in small plots—beans and yams, manioc and cabbage. As the Marines passed through the village and into this area the sound of small-arms fire grew in volume. In one sense it was a relief, for although this was mid-1965 none of our efforts to that time had flushed the elusive

Main Force Viet Cong. We knew they existed, that they controlled much of the rural population, and that they were the main support of the local guerrilla. We didn't know, yet, how good they were in a fight.

When our Marines had come sufficiently to grips with the enemy force inland, the picture became more clear: for the first time we had surprised the Viet Cong. They had fled the village area precipitantly, chasing the villagers before them so that none could give us any information. We moved too fast for them, and they had to turn and fight in hastily prepared positions not far inland. There were about a hundred of them, roughly a company of troops. This first contact confirmed somewhat the various rumors and facts that had brought us to this hot, dusty peninsula. But we were after a bigger target than a Viet Cong company.

The temperature was soaring over a hundred when I flew out of the beach area to the inland hills where our helicopter-borne troops were landing in a great semicircle, the outer ring of the big trap we were emplacing. They too came under fire early in the landing, but this time from the shoreward side. It was hot, dirty fighting. The earth was very dry, and the helicopters put up clouds of red dust at each landing and takeoff. Everyone was quickly covered with a coat of dust that became plastered to the body by sweat. Yet there was an almost visible emotional surge forward. All of us began to realize that we had cornered a major Viet Cong force; that it was fighting inland from the beach to escape our amphibious assault, and that its forward elements had already been stopped by the Marines landed by helicopters so well inland.

The battle developed quickly and we soon felt the sting of the Main Force Viet Cong.

There has always been something a little pathetic about the local guerrilla force, principally because of the extreme youth of many of its members (the Viet Cong conscript villagers as young as thirteen), the occasional young girl, the often inadequate weapons. There was nothing pathetic about the Main Force. These were hard-bitten troops, no youngsters among them. They asked for no quarter, and fought efficiently and sometimes fanatically.

They had picked a good place to make their initial stand. As the fight developed we began to see its pattern. This was hedgerow country, between the beach and the ring of low hills inland where our helicopter-borne forces were landing. Each family plot was bordered by a row of cactus, thorn, brush, and bamboo. The tangled roots of the vegetation produced low but solid mounds of earth along each row—almost perfect cover and concealment for a defending force. The plots were small enough to allow the defender to leapfrog back to the next row if pressure on him got too great, but large enough to give open fields of fire against the attacking force as it attempted to move. The Army had encountered this same difficulty in Normandy; now their sons fought through it once again, twenty years and seven thousand miles away.

As the rifle companies moved inland from the beach and down from the hills into this checkerboard of hedge and field, they entered the close, savage type of combat that marks the infantry battle. There are no rules here but club and fang; no referee except the victor; no score but win or lose.

As always when the tempo of the fighting increased, the calls for support became more imperative, and every means at our disposal was thrown into that blazing edge where the outcome would be decided. Artillery and the naval guns offshore, Marine aircraft from Chu Lai and Danang, rocket, bomb, and shell, were there and used, and still the fighting raged. The calls came in for more ammunition and water, water, water as the temperature reached a hundred and ten and the tired men fought deeper into the roadless country.

The Marines have amphibian vehicles for much of their initial assault supplies. Preloaded aboard the ships, they swim in on call, across the beaches and inland on their tracks. We used them, and the Viet Cong unleashed a weapon we knew they had, but hadn't encountered until that time—a powerful little recoilless rifle, fired from the shoulder or from a simple ground mount. Made in Communist China, this weapon quickly showed it could penetrate the armor of a medium tank, and easily knock out an amphibian tractor with its light steel hull.

The first ones we brought ashore—five tractors with an escort of two tanks—were hit only a couple of hundred yards in rear of the company they were supplying. The rifle company went to their aid but received heavy fire itself, and a particularly heavy fight developed around the vehicles. Units were shifted to continue the movement inland while the one company continued to engage the Viet Cong who had denied them their supplies.

This well-armed enemy unit had appeared at a curious point of the battle, themselves moving toward the beach as the Marines moved inland. It is most likely, and I have always felt it to be certain, that they were striking toward our main command post, just inland from the fishing village, when they encountered the tank and tractor column maneuvering forward through the hedgerows. These Viet Cong had rocket launchers as well as recoilless rifles, mortars, and plenty of automatic weapons. They could have done great damage in the beach area if they had not accepted the target they encountered on the way. These were bold men, and they acted on a decision made in the heat of battle—there were no survivors who could tell us how or why.

In spite of this new threat—the effectiveness of their small but potent antitank gun—more tanks moved in from the offshore ships, lightered into the beach by the Navy and working up into the battlefront to cover the infantry with their big steel bodies and their guns, firing from hedgerow with cannon and machine gun, the same type of tank-infantry team that broke through the hedgerows of Normandy.

There was another team in action—our Marine Corps air-ground team—and it also paid off. Under control of Marine aviators accompanying the troops on the ground the jets made bombing and strafing runs within yards of the advancing troops. Here, the hedgerows helped, neat lines penciled on the ground, marked by our own tracer fire or colored smoke as a Viet Cong firing line. Our jets would shriek in, guns blazing, and unload their bombs moments before the ground troops assaulted across the open fields or along the hedgerows leading to the target.

Marine pilots also used the hedgerows as cover for their helicopters, bringing them in a row or two behind the forward edge of battle to unload water and ammunition and take on the wounded men. Aid stations, except for the simplest of battle dressings, were not required—helicopters lifted the men from the very field in which they had been hit and lofted them to the Navy hospital at Chu Lai in minutes, each man perhaps owing his life to the guts of a Marine helicopter crew that flew through fire each time, in and out, from dawn to after dark, landing in the circle of hand-held flashlights or the faint blue corner markers of the helicopter landing site.

As the battle went on elements of the helicopter-borne force inland and the amphibious force on the shore side joined. Sun-darkened little men in black pajamas tried to stop the closing of our forces around them. When in spite of all their efforts the ring around them joined, they did not panic, but tried to break through. They had mortars and machine guns and they used them well. They attacked in mass, firing automatic weapons as they advanced. Finally, in desperation, but still without panic, they attacked in columns, firing to right and left as well as to the front, some getting through to flee inland, some dying in the attempt. One group, pressed against the sea, clambered down the low cliffs and tried to get out by sampan, the little fishing boats that dotted the beaches, and there the Navy caught them with fire from the destroyers and the cruiser offshore.

To their credit, few surrendered.

When it was over, the fields and the beaches were strewn with their bodies, more than six hundred of them. The rest were either deep in hidden burrows or had gotten inland, to lick their wounds in the hills and contemplate the power of American arms. It was many months before we heard from the Main Force Viet Cong in that area again, and ever after that they kept their backs to the mountains, not the sea. Both of us had learned from our first major encounter.

We had learned that our overwhelming superiority in weapons and supporting arms denied the enemy any chance of victory in a conventional battle situation; that the mobility of the helicopter more than offset his knowledge of the ground and quick movement; that our ability to land by sea denied him a series of sanctuaries along the coast he had used for years as rest areas, assembly points, and bases supplied from the sea. We had also learned that his 57-millimeter recoilless cannons would knock out a medium tank or amphibian tractor with ease; that he was something better than good, and usually superb in battle.

The lessons the enemy learned were even more significant. Primarily, it had been demonstrated beyond all doubt that they were in a completely different circumstance than had existed in their fight against the Republic of Vietnam; that no longer could they roam freely over the countryside or hold bases along the coast, where the bulk of the people lived. From this point on, their effect on the villagers and their support of the local guerrillas were on the wane. Heretofore, the Main Force had been Big Brother to the local guerrillas. It had provided them with a powerful clout against targets they were too weak to attack by themselves, against government forces who were gaining an upper hand over them, and against the people themselves when they turned against the guerrilla and his methods. From now on the hills and mountains into which the Main Force had been driven would increasingly become their home, and they would increasingly abandon the local guerrilla to his lonely fight against the government.

This was the pattern, from the summer of 1965 for almost another year. Time after time we identified and closed with the Main Force Viet Cong, each time a little farther back into the mountains or farther north toward the Demilitarized Zone. They became weaker as the difficulties of supplying them in the mountains increased, as their men contracted malaria, as the food and human resources of the coast were increasingly denied them. By the end of 1965 they were telling the guerrillas, "We can no longer help you; it is we who need your help. It is now your battle, for we can no longer come down from the hills lest we perish."

This was a turning point. From this time on, no Viet Cong regiment or battalion would ever score a significant success against our forces in I Corps.

So we turned to the guerrilla and the sea of people in which he lived. A steel gauntlet had closed on the Main Force and forced him back into the mountains, but we could not—nor did we wish to—do this to a people. The guerrilla had somehow to be strained out of the mass of the populace. This called for strange, unprecedented tactics for groups of fighting men. It required a gentler touch, the sensitive feel of a velvet glove.

7

Velvet Glove

Doan Van Hoa was only ten years old, but he was the head of a family. His father had been killed by the Viet Cong and his shocked mother had become a recluse since her husband's death. There were eight children, from a naked baby to Doan, the eldest son. In the custom of the Orient, Doan received the respect of the others and took the burden of responsibility on his thin shoulders. It was even harder for him than for others in like circumstances—and there were many—because Doan had been crippled by polio.

The family barely survived. There was shelter of sorts, enough to shield them from the worst sun and hardest rain. There was always food somewhere in their lush land, but never enough for all nine mouths. Clothing was too much a luxury to be considered, so they wore such tattered rags as covered their nakedness and gave some protection from sun and chill and rain, and that served as bedclothes too, when the long nights began and the cookfires of more fortunate families looked rich and warm in the darkness.

Little Doan limped about in a constant search for a mouthful of food, a scrap of wood to add to their hut, or a castoff rag for their clothing. He was in the town when the Americans came,

Velvet Glove

and he watched them with bright, intelligent eyes. He saw their inconceivable wealth and fantastic machines. He noted their immense size, and marked in his mind that they were constantly busy, with brusque manners, but were not unkind.

Doan was destitute, but he was no beggar. Even though these huge strangers wasted much that he could use, he could not ask for it nor scramble with his withered limbs against the other children who picked each refuse heap clean of usables. Doan waited and watched and thought it out with his keen young mind, meanwhile picking up a few phrases of the foreigners' strange, toneless speech.

One day he saw one close at hand, standing in the village, almost the first one he had seen not frantically busy at doing something. Cautiously Doan approached, trying not to limp. With the charming directness of a child and the natural dignity of a Vietnamese, he posed a question—in English: "American, you be my friend?"

Cpl. Ronald W. Field looked down at the ragged, filthy little boy and into his grave eyes. He didn't answer at once, but studied him for some time. Doan phrased the question again, carefully enunciating the words as he had learned them, hoping he had the strange sound correct. Cautiously, seriously, Corporal Field answered : "Yeah, I'll be your friend." Doan smiled, as only a boy of ten can smile, reached up and took the Marine's big hand. Together they walked down the dusty street, one of them small, limping, and hopeful, one of them big, powerful, cautious, and puzzled, like the two nations they represented.

In Vietnam all but a very few of the people are in what in the United States would be called a "low-income group." As in our own country there are the special problems of the aged and the handicapped, the underemployed, and the very young. The long war has added millions of displaced persons and refugees, tens of thousands of orphans and disabled.

[79]

Velvet Glove

When we entered the country, we were faced with these problems in a very real sense. There was no time for research, test programs, surveys, or studies. The plight of the people was written on their faces and in the children's swollen bellies. So we acted, not always wisely, not always well, but always with good intent.

We went among the people to ask them what they wanted, and they answered simply and directly, for they are a simple and direct people: Peace; a chance to grow what we need to eat and sell what we do not need ourselves; a chance to buy what we cannot grow or make; a chance for our children to be something more than what we are; relief from our pains; cures for our ills; something to help us in the grinding labor that is our life, and was the life of our fathers, and will be the life of our sons.

We could not give them peace, not yet, but we could offer security from Viet Cong attack and restraint in our own actions. As for the other desires, the needs were so great that there was no problem finding what to do.

I don't recall when I first realized that the guerrilla can never afford to wear a velvet glove. It was sometime during our first attempts to help the people who, for all we knew, were Viet Cong themselves. That we could be enemies at night and friends in the daytime was another peculiarity of this war; but to a guerrilla force such a circumstance would be a disaster. The guerrilla's survival depends upon a population either friendly toward him or sufficiently under control by other means to provide him with the cooperation and support he needs.

Such control over the people must be absolute to be effective. One or two individuals in a village can destroy him with a whisper in the night. For men living under this fear, an attitude of benevolence is not enough. Because their lives are in the balance, their rule is harsh, their punishments swift and severe,

Velvet Glove

often unjust and often self-defeating. Che Guevara learned this in the Bolivian mountains; the Viet Cong have learned it, too. So have the people of Vietnam. The most obvious result is the flood of refugees to a more benign rule than that imposed by the guerrillas. But there are less conspicuous results: malingering and slowdown, the hiding of produce and evasion from conscription, apathy and sullenness—and the insidious leakage of information that can ultimately destroy the guerrilla force.

Much nonsense has been written about guerrilla warfare. It has almost become a cult. I much prefer the hard good sense of one of the great practitioners: "It [guerrilla warfare] must have a friendly population, not actively friendly, but sympathetic to the point of not betraying rebel movements to the enemy. Rebellions can be made by 2 percent active in a striking force, and 98 percent passively sympathetic." *

This necessity of 100-per-cent active or passive support from the population is the Achilles' heel of the guerrilla. With such support he is a hero and a patriot. Without it he is a bandit, controlling by terror, or a quisling, betraying his own people to a foreign interest. These are men to be dreaded, as the Viet Cong are dreaded by the Vietnamese. They can destroy, but they cannot build; they fear benevolence because they themselves are despots.

To those of us who saw the suffering of the Vietnamese people, benevolence was its own reward, but it was more: it was a weapon against the guerrilla that he could not use himself without unacceptable risk; it was also a way to shorten the war that was the cause of the suffering. Our response has borne many names: Revolutionary Development, Civic Action, Civil Affairs, Revolutionary Warfare. The name doesn't matter, the idea does: sympathy, understanding, regard for the people.

Perhaps we could have done better, but what we did worked. The bonds between us—the Americans and the Viet-

* T. E. Lawrence, *Encyclopaedia Britannica*, 1947.

namese people—grew, thread by thread; so did the bonds between them and their own government. Not without blunders or problems; but they grew nevertheless, in deep contrast to what the Viet Cong were losing—the sympathy of the people.

The response was not immediate, but it also grew, as the children warned us of booby traps, the women showed us where the rice was stored for the Viet Cong, the elders told us when the Viet Cong would come to collect their taxes or hold their next meeting. Sometimes it was a guarded communication. I remember when a young Naval doctor told us that the villagers had warned him against his next visit—to come not on the scheduled day but the day after. No mention of the Viet Cong, but the message was clear.

None of this was easy, and the resources were far less than the almost limitless demand upon them. It rapidly devolved to fundamentals. What do you do for over a million people who lack almost everything?

The doctor told us: most of the suffering is a product of uncleanliness, not because these people are unclean by nature, but because they have no soap. So we gave them soap, through their own leaders or directly, until we ran short. We asked the American people to give us soap, and they responded with soap by the ton. A small thing in itself, but large to the scabic child, the farmer who tears his flesh each day in the rich muck of the paddies, the American who sees their suppurating sores.

Many were hungry, and we fed them. Many were almost naked, and we clothed them. Many were ill, and we gave them care.

We found that the war had disrupted the traditional crafts of the village, and that skills such as masonry, carpentry, and metalsmithing still existed as family trades—as they had for a thousand years or more—but the artisans lacked the basic tools to follow their profession. Their saws, hammers, anvils, or trowels

Velvet Glove

had long since been confiscated to be melted down into weapons.

Until we were better advised by our Vietnamese counterparts, we first thought of making another plea to the American people, this time for craft tools. We were made to realize, however, that a tool made for a hundred-and-eighty-pound American was not an efficient instrument in the hands of a ninety-pound Vietnamese. As a single example, the beefy American carpenter cuts a board with the forward stroke of his saw with one hand; the lighter Asian cuts on the pull stroke with a two-handed saw. There are similar, but equally fundamental, differences with other tools.

One answer came from the Marine Corps Reserve. They had not been called to active duty for the war in Vietnam; yet they felt as deeply involved as we who were there. Through them we received huge donated funds we could use in the Far East for the direct purchase of tools made for Asians by Asians, for carpenters and masons, midwives and seamstresses, blacksmiths and farmers. They came into Vietnam as complete kits, from Taiwan and Korea and Japan, and went to the villages where families who already knew every aspect of their trade accepted them and went to work within the same day—not beggars, not public wards, but artisans anxious and willing to ply their own trades. We couldn't have done it without help—not only of the Marine Corps Reserve but also of CARE, which purchased the tools for us, shipped them, and helped us distribute them in Vietnam.

We leaned heavily on others for support in this strange new role: religious organizations that collected and helped us distribute food and clothing to the people; the International Rescue Committee, which obtained huge quantities of donated medicines desperately needed by the people; International Orphans, Inc., which cared for thousands of distressed children in our behalf; HOPE, HANDCLASP, and more than twenty other organizations.

In spite of such welcome support, we—the Marines—felt quite alone initially in the huge effort we were putting into what was then called Civic Action. There was a war on and we were fighting it as well as were all others. We were also fighting that other war in which gains were not measured in ground taken, "body count," or the number of weapons captured; in which gains were not really measurable at all. The number of wells dug, the number of patients treated could be tabulated, but the meaning of them to the Vietnamese people, the results of these works in the myriad ways they could be evidenced were immeasurable. It may have been unscientific, but the gut feeling was there and we followed it through.

It wasn't long until the Marine Corps operations in Vietnam were particularly marked by social and economic betterment of the people. It was not that we were just doing more than fighting. There was no single dramatic event at which our success became obvious; rather, it grew from hundreds of thousands of little acts of good will.

There is a village near our Chu Lai base, originally a cluster of huts in the sand and scrub of that rather desolate area. Over the years dozens of Marine units have come and gone; thousands of men have done their duty in Vietnam and returned home—and each has left behind something of himself. When last I saw that village, there were more than seven hundred neat homes along broad, graded roads. Both a Buddhist temple and a Catholic church stood at the center of the community. There were three hundred and fifty students in the village school, a clinic manned by American-trained Vietnamese nurses, a communal pig farm, village warehouse, and granary. An artificial lake, stocked with fish and ducks, softened the glare of sand and sun and watered the villagers' green gardens. Here, I thought, was a useful "body count"—three thousand

Velvet Glove

healthy, secure people, living decently, with hope for the future.

There was a hamlet of Hoa Khanh, four thousand people scratching out a living on poor, sandy soil. After the Marines came and the Viet Cong fled or were rooted out, Hoa Khanh was inundated by a sea of refugees from other areas seeking safety from the Vietnamese communists and a chance to live their own lives. They came with what they could carry or wear, and the population of Hoa Khanh swelled to ten thousand. The new arrivals were ragged and filthy, hungry and diseased; the original population was not much better off. These were good people, in need of succor, and they got it from men whose normal working day was sixteen hours or more, who lived in daily danger from the Viet Cong, yet found the time and energy and will to help.

It isn't hard to know where to start when everything is needed, when there is a one-room school shack for twenty-five hundred children, when there isn't enough food or clothing to go around, when there aren't enough shelters for half the people, when you can see the eyes gummed with mucus, and the boils and ulcers on the bodies, the ringworm glistening on the flesh, and the bellies of children swollen with intestinal worms.

Hoa Khanh not only survived, it thrived. Simple huts of bamboo frame and thatch of rush or straw encompass the original town, homes built by the refugees with their own hands. There are sixteen classrooms, not just one, all good, sound buildings of solid masonry, cool and well ventilated, built by the people themselves with Marine help. A hundred and fifty people a day troop through the new clinic, being treated, free, for ailments that used to be left until their flesh was rotted and their bodies debilitated.

Hoa Khanh still cannot grow its own food, but it has turned its barren, sandy soil into an asset rather than a liability. The village trade is now brickmaking: hand-rammed, sun-dried bricks of sand and cement are exchanged with other communities for rice or other produce. The simple machines needed were bought by the Marines with money donated by the Marine Corps Reserve in the United States, those men and women not on active duty but actively in the war in their own meaningful way. Each month the cement comes from the same source. There is no great show; just people helping people, and not always does the real feeling come to the surface.

It did in Hoa Khanh, once, when Second Lt. Irwin Waldvogel of Grayslake, Illinois, who had first organized help for them, was about to go home, and he received a letter from the village chief that read in part:

> Our village know that you will return home to your country. Our village committee as well as all the villagers thank you for your help. . . . Hoa Khanh village committee as well as its villagers love him who is always considered as foster brother. We are deeply truly grateful to him. We and approximately 9,500 villagers thank you very much. . . .

It was late in 1965 that I first met Le Thuc Can.

We had heard through our increasing number of Vietnamese friends that a Viet Cong battalion was off in the hills some twenty miles southwest of Danang, and we were soon off to seek them out. It was an odd area, deep into what we then considered enemy territory. There was a river to the north and a range of hills to the south. West, the country rose into the foothills of the central mountain range that stretched into Laos.

In this general triangle was a fertile plain once claimed by the Republic of Vietnam as a strategic hamlet area. It was much more than that. Since World War II, the inhabitants had dug into the rich soil with increasingly elaborate underground shelter, storage caves, and connecting tunnels that went thousands of yards from hamlet to hamlet and even from village to village. Originally designed to protect the people and their produce from the vicissitudes of war, these had been carefully plotted by the Viet Cong and increasingly used by them since 1960.

Most of all, there was a prize there: the only coal mine in the Republic of Vietnam and a natural basin where hydroelectric power could be generated. The potential was enormous. Here, within twenty miles of Danang, was power for electricity and heat, for light industry and fertilizer production and water purification, all in one concentrated area.

This had been recognized by the government of the Republic of Vietnam four years before. The whole industrial complex had been nearing completion in early 1965. All that remained to be done was to construct buildings to house the hydroelectric plant, the water purification plant, and the chemical fertilizer plant. The plant equipment was either in Saigon or in Europe, awaiting shipment. But the Viet Cong severed the road to Danang and stopped the construction of a railroad spur between the city and the proposed industrial complex.

Le Thuc Can was an engineer. He had spent ten years in France earning his degree and six months in Ohio and Pennsylvania learning strip-mining methods. He had come back to Vietnam in 1961, prepared to devote his life's energies to his people. I met him in An Hoa, the hub of his project, four years later. I have rarely met a more dedicated, sincere, or competent man in over half a century of living.

When the road to the coast was cut, Le Thuc Can had an airstrip built. As his requirements mounted, he expanded the airfield from five hundred to a thousand feet, then to fifteen hundred feet, and finally to three thousand feet. He collected twenty-five engineers, all Vietnamese, all but one educated in

Vietnam. He brought in young peasant boys and set up training schools where they learned the skills of electricians, welders, and mechanics for the day they would be needed.

When the Viet Cong threatened him, Le Thuc Can helped organize a civilian guard force to supplement the thin government garrison in the area. For his own people Le Thuc Can provided comfortable cottages and laid out plans for an ultimate community of five thousand or more.

We encountered this solid little knot of competent, hardworking people while hunting down a Viet Cong battalion; encountered Le Thuc Can and the twenty-five other engineers and a thousand or more people trained or being trained as artisans and technicians, young people all, in their twenties and thirties—this in the middle of Viet Cong country.

There was something else peculiar about the An Hoa area. Villagers well separated from the industrial complex led us to Viet Cong rice, weapons, and ammunition caches, showed us their dugouts and tunnels—some more than three thousand yards long—and joined us when we left. More than four thousand came out with us the first time we entered the An Hoa area, carrying their household goods on their backs, swimming their water buffalo across rivers, knowing they could not load their families on Mr. Can's industrial area without destroying all he had done and unwilling to remain one more day under domination of the Viet Cong.

We came back to An Hoa before too long, this time to stay. It took a little longer than we thought, but we also punched a road through from Danang to An Hoa and called it "Liberty Road." We meant it.

What we have done in Vietnam will not be measured in tons of bombs or shells, the dismal count of young men's bodies on the battlefield, or the number of wells dug or market places built. I sought in vain for some yardstick by which to appraise progress in this kind of war and found none adequate.

I know this: half a million meals a month into the mouths of famished people is not wrong; ministering to the sick and injured is not wrong; lightening their awful load of labor is not wrong. I know that every child we put in school is to our common good, and every teacher, nurse, or artisan we train transmits his knowledge through a generation if we can keep him from being butchered by the Viet Cong because he is a man of good will.

I have watched impatiently the slow but steady increase in voluntary acts by the Vietnamese people that indicate the real success of what we have done: the incidents when they assist us in finding the Viet Cong, their weapons and supplies; the rate at which the local guerrillas, the sons and brothers of villagers, surrender of their own free will; the gradual transition of communities from hostile to apathetic to friendly.

I remember the young Viet Cong, still a boy, who had come down out of the hills on his first mission, fired with enthusiasm to drive the hated invader from his country and free his people from the vicious oppression of the American colonialists. He knew what to expect and he looked for it: his people under the lash of the foreigner. The first American he saw was waist-deep in muck, fitting the underpinnings of a small footbridge, laughing and joking with the villagers, all of them working together; and the American was doing the hardest and dirtiest task. At that time and place we won a segment of the war, and not with bullets.

That was one enemy soldier, at one spot, several years ago. If we are to end the war in Vietnam, or any such war anywhere else, with justice to the men who fought it in the name of their own country, then it must be won among the people, not against them. The communist world may talk of revolution, but we have such a revolution to offer as would make their doctrinaire minds reel. It involves individual dignity and the pride of family, national independence and self-determination; it is called Freedom. The Vietnamese south of the Demilitarized Zone are fighting for it now. They call it *Doc-Lap*—Independence. For without that they can be no more free than their brothers to the north.

8

Doc-Lap!

Since I came home the question has been posed to me many times: Why don't the Vietnamese fight for their own country, as we are fighting for them? I answer, and it is hard for people to believe the answer. Few Americans I have met can realize the awful toll in lives expended by a nation of 17 million people over the past few years alone:

Prior to 1966—more than thirty thousand dead soldiers, sailors, and airmen;

1966—eleven thousand dead soldiers, sailors, and airmen;

1967—twelve thousand dead soldiers, sailors, and airmen;

1968—seventeen thousand dead soldiers, sailors, and airmen; fifty-seven thousand wounded; more than two thousand missing in action;

1969—twenty-two thousand dead soldiers, sailors, and airmen; sixty-five thousand wounded; more than nine hundred missing in action.

To give even more meaning to these figures: If the percentage were compared to our own population, it would mean that more than a million men would have died in action, not to mention millions wounded. You do not die on this scale by staying close to Saigon or by huddling in a bunker somewhere waiting for the Americans to fight your battle. These ninety-two thousand men died in the field, fighting for their country as we have fought for ours, and as they themselves have fought before. The history of Vietnam is one of conflict, and only those who know the Vietnamese least discount their quality and reputation as warriors.

Before our involvement in Vietnam we knew practically nothing of its people. As late as 1958 there was no history of them printed in the English language. There are only two or three today, none widely read.

The appearance and manner of the Vietnamese are in themselves disarming. It comes as a surprise that these charming people can fight like demons. The Vietnamese are furiously proud, infinitely patient, and solidly opposed to interference. They have demonstrated these traits for thousands of years. They have unusual strength, the product of a long history of hardship, war, and suffering.

The very origin of the Vietnamese was a struggle against the environment of their earliest homeland—the Red River Valley delta, what is now Hanoi and Haiphong. Here, thousands of years ago, they settled into a region that was fertile but inimical to human life. The irregularity of rains caused periods of starving drought and of raging flood. A man or a family could not defeat this vast cycle of dry and wet monsoon, but a people could. From early times a characteristic developed—cooperation, unity, the coordination of human effort against a hostile world. There also developed pride—pride in having won against the elements, pride in being strong, intelligent, enduring.

The Vietnamese, when France was called Gaul and the Britons wore animal skins, already had a high degree of civilization and cultural unity. Today, divided politically, they remain identical physically and speak one language from the Chinese border to the Mekong Delta.

Doc-Lap!

The mixture of tribes, languages, and customs that marks the mountain regions are separate from the mainstream of Vietnam. The Vietnamese are lowland people—their backs to the mountains, their faces toward the sea, and their energies devoted to the lush paddylands such as marked their original homeland beside the Red River. In this environment the Vietnamese became skilled seamen, marrying the salt- and protein-rich products of the sea to their basic rice diet. With ample timber in the mountains for fuel and building material, the bounty of the sea at hand, and the abundant grain harvest of the floodplains, the Vietnamese thrived and expanded southward until they occupied the other great delta area that balances the south with the north—the mouth of the Mekong River. None of this occurred without enormous human effort and tragic opposition.

First, the control of the Red River. To harness the waters, the Vietnamese built a fantastic system of dikes and hydraulic controls. Before the first Caesar they had constructed fifteen hundred miles of dikes by hand and basket, instituted a communal system of watches, and established community organizations for emergency repairs. All of these works were beyond the capability of the basic family unit. To effect them, the Vietnamese organized on the village level a stable social community for the common good. This structure marks the Vietnamese throughout their history: close family relationships, groups of families in hamlets, groups of hamlets in villages, and regional cooperation.

The initial wealth and prosperity that came to the Vietnamese through labor and organization brought the first of an unending series of human catastrophes.

Two thousand years ago the Chinese, coveting the rich ricelands, moved powerfully down from the north in a series of invasions. The Vietnamese, as they have always done, fought the invader. For a hundred years, four generations, they held out against the hordes of China, outnumbered, seeing their lands laid waste, watching their treasuries sink. Finally the grandsons of the original armies succumbed, exhausted, and Vietnam (Nam Viet at the time) became a Chinese province. For a thousand years thereafter the Vietnamese lived under Chinese rule. For a thousand years they continued to resist the invaders. Defeat after defeat did not still the revolt or submit the nation to foreign assimilation. For the villages remained Vietnamese. While the Chinese ruled the country, the villages held to the old customs, maintained the old religions, celebrated the old festivals, raised their children as Vietnamese, and taught them to despise the invaders.

The struggle came to a climax in the tenth century. Vietnamese resistance armies rose in quick succession against a weakening and deteriorating China. Finally the Chinese were driven out, and Vietnam stood independent once more. But the great menace of China remained, and the weight of her armies was felt repeatedly. Sometimes the Vietnamese went down in defeat, and Chinese rule was reimposed, but always briefly. The Vietnamese, hardened in a thousand years of battle, seemed to gain in national vigor at each new trial by arms.

Then came Kublai Khan. The master of the greatest Asian empire ever seen, he sent half a million Mongols down upon the Red River Valley in 1284. The whole people were embattled. Small-statured men, tiny women, children, old men and women, hamlet by hamlet and family by family. The Mongol army was decimated by this furious, common stand—a stunning victory by an aroused and united people. But the toll was heavy, and a weakened Vietnam could not indefinitely stand against the full might of China. So when the Ming Dynasty, still coveting the rich ricelands of Nam Viet, invaded the country with another vast army, the Vietnamese found themselves again defeated, exhausted, under Chinese rule.

The efficient Mings ground down the Vietnamese with oppressive taxation and siphoned off millions of men in forced labor to cut the forests and dig the mines. But they did not reckon with the tenacity of the Vietnamese, who developed a resistance movement and for ten years so harassed the Chinese rulers that they were forced again to evacuate the country. This experience, and mounting troubles in the homeland, quieted the northern colossus, and the Vietnamese found themselves, for the first time, with generations of independence and security.

It is typical of the Vietnamese that they responded to this period by unparalleled exploitation and expansion. Vigorous, industrious, venturesome, proud, and capable, they pushed rapidly south, soldier-farmers and soldier-fishermen, from valley to valley and river to river. The Song Ca, the Ca De Song, the Song Vu Gia, the Song Tra Bong, all the broad paddylands, rich in the sun, came quickly under the efficient hands and alert intelligence of the Vietnamese until the final prize—the magnificent delta of the Mekong, as vast and fertile as the original homeland in the Red River Valley—was won. Vietnam was whole: two vast rice baskets balanced on a bridge of hardy, competent people stretched along a thousand miles of coast.

Then a new human catastrophe began. From the sea came bearded, rank-smelling men with powerful new weapons and strange, efficient ways. The Portuguese first, then the Dutch, the English, and the French. At first it was a mercantile invasion, and the Europeans fought each other while the Vietnamese watched and waited. After that the Vietnamese saw alien religions planted by the newcomers; little colonies established, based on new churches, protected by the powerful ships and forming focal points for increased trade.

Gradually, as the influence of the French forced out the other European competitors, the independent country of Vietnam faced its next conquerer. In 1858 the French seized Tourane (Danang) and later Saigon. Not surprisingly, the people

[95]

fought back, but this was not like the old wars. The powerful new weapons and tight European discipline far overmatched the swords of the Vietnamese.

Faced with this new strength, the Emperor Tu Do capitulated and ceded to French rule the three provinces surrounding Saigon. The people of Vietnam, however, did not surrender. Ignoring their ruler, they took up the fight with the only means they had remaining—guerrilla war against the invader. It was a cruel time. By 1867 France had seized the entire area south of Saigon: the rich Mekong Delta, basis for vast plantations and millions of landless peasants. In 1883 France seized the other great valley area to the north: the Red River, Haiphong, and Hanoi. Then began a dozen years of incessant war against the desperately resisting population, and eventual subjugation of the original Nam Viet homeland.

The announcement of old Emperor Tu Do's death is perhaps the best expression of this hard time: "He was killed by sorrow to see the foreigners invade his empire; and he died with curses on his lips. Keep him in your hearts and avenge his memory."

For a generation the Vietnamese openly fought the French and were defeated by modern arms. Hopelessly, they went underground, formed a government in exile, and fomented insurrections at every opportunity. They took lessons from Chiang Kai-shek and formed a nationalist party movement (VNQDD, or *Viet-Nam Quoc Dan Dang*) modeled on the Chinese Nationalist Kuomintang. It still exists today. They took lessons from the communists and formed a Communist Party of Indochina. They rebelled—1913, 1915, 1917, 1930.

They endured the occupation of their country by the Japanese during World War II, first with the agreement of the French (Vichy) Government. From 1940, a year before Pearl Harbor, to 1945, the Japanese Army had free use of all Indochinese cities, ports, and airfields, exercising increasing control of the country through the war years. By the end of the war the

Doc-Lap!

Japanese had disarmed and interned all the French military units in Vietnam and placed most of the French government officials under arrest.

After the capitulation of Japan there appeared to be hope for the people. During the last months of the war the Japanese had allowed the traditional ruler, Emperor Bao Dai, to proclaim the independence of Vietnam. Various nationalist groups—including the *Mat Tran Viet-Nam Doc-Lap Dong-Minh,* or Viet Minh—began to operate openly after the long years of suppression. A scholar, Tran Trong Kim, was made premier of the country and formed a government at the traditional capital of Hué. The preparation of a constitution began, based on a united Vietnam and political and religious freedom. Fiscal reforms were announced that exempted citizens who did not own property from personal income tax. A national youth movement was organized; the schools began to teach the Vietnamese language instead of French; political prisoners and exiles were given amnesty. Vietnam was becoming Vietnamese again.

Then this hope was wrecked. The breakdown began with Ho Chi Minh and his Viet Minh Party, now armed and in the open. Their flag was flown in Hanoi and their stormtroopers occupied the major public buildings. Other nationalist groups were driven into hiding by armed bands or forced to join the Viet Minh movement. The Japanese were left alone; to Ho Chi Minh the enemy was the non-communist Vietnamese.

Quickly—in one week—Vietnam was torn apart again. The Viet Minh controlled the north from Hanoi; the new government in Hué fell; a provisional government of communists established itself in Saigon as the "Provisional Executive Committee of South Vietnam."

The Viet Minh regime was well organized and ruthless. It struck at the heart of Vietnamese society by replacing the village councils with "People's Committees." A militia force was established. The young people were organized into training groups for indoctrination and development into "Resistance Committees" at the village level. A regular army was built up from the large number of experienced soldiers remaining from the recent World War.

In spite of these actions, the government established by Ho Chi Minh was weak. It was politically unstable as yet, a minority exercising control over the majority by threat and coercion. It was militarily feeble, with a raw militia and an army containing many potentially unreliable elements and men. Soon it faced its own crisis, and the Vietnamese people entered another long agony. Only two weeks after Ho Chi Minh proclaimed his "Democratic Government," foreign troops again moved into Vietnam.

It was one month since Japan had capitulated. The Japanese Army had stopped fighting, but it still was in Vietnam, still armed, still situated in all the major cities, ports, and airfields of the country. On September 12, 1945, British troops began landing in South Vietnam and Nationalist Chinese troops began entering North Vietnam, to disarm and return the Japanese forces to their homeland. This was their mission and they accomplished it.

During their presence, however, another factor entered: They were joined by French troops—units of the Free French forces who had fought on the Allied side until the defeat of Germany and Japan. As the Japanese, the British, and the Chinese forces departed from Vietnam, the French forces remained. In the north they occupied the government palace, and the Vietnamese people saw it as the symbolic as well as the actual resumption of French colonial rule. Quietly, firmly, in the Vietnamese manner, they closed ranks behind Ho Chi Minh and his thirty thousand Viet Minh and endured one more decade of bloodshed, more terrible this time than World War

II had been for them. The Indochina War was under way.

The rest is recent history, although most of the young men fighting in Vietnam today were only two or three years old when the defeated French finally withdrew from Vietnam. In 1954 Vietnam again declared its independence, and hostilities ended with the signatures of a French Brigadier General and a Vietnamese Vice-Minister of National Defense in Geneva, Switzerland.

Our memory is sometimes dim on these Geneva Accords. In one sense they recognize Vietnam as a single people and as a single nation; in another they divide it between north and south, between communism and the Free World. The nation we now know as the Republic of Vietnam did not sign the document at Geneva in 1954; neither did any representative of the United States of America.

The government of the Republic of Vietnam could not and did not accept the manifestly unfavorable terms under which a unified election was set for 1956, under the supervision of an international commission composed of members from India, Poland, and Canada. The commission had already made clear its impotence in the face of open and massive communist violations of the Geneva Agreements.

A free and fair election was physically impossible in the communist half of Vietnam and in the large southern regions controlled by the Viet Cong. The northern citizenry was under a one-party totalitarian discipline, whereas the electorate in the south, even where communist domination was only partial, was honeycombed by Viet Cong terrorists and wide open to communist propaganda and threats. In these circumstances an election would have been farcical—no more than a ritual for turning all of Vietnam over to communism. Only if it was ready for a thinly camouflaged surrender could the Saigon leadership have approved the election. And it definitely was not.

Doc-Lap!

The ink was hardly dry on the Geneva settlement dividing the country at the 17th Parallel, it should be remembered, when the communists in the north announced their intention to "unify" the area—by force if necessary. "All the peoples and soldiers of the North and South must unite to conquer victory," Ho Chi Minh announced on July 22, 1954—hardly a call for free elections. Under instructions from Hanoi between five and ten thousand communist-trained guerrillas remained in the south, and were joined by thousands more infiltrated with the flood of refugees from North Vietnam.

All of these secret and illegal forces were deployed, with arms and munitions cached for use when Hanoi should give the signal. In the ten months between July 1955 and May 1956 the southern government rounded up more than fifteen thousand northern agents and uncovered seven hundred caches of arms, evidence of Hanoi's intervention—in defiance of the Geneva rules—even at that early stage. This was the time bomb planted in the south for detonation from the north: nucleus of the National Liberation Front, the Army of Liberation, the Viet Cong, all false fronts for the ruling party in the north.

From 1958 onward Hanoi was openly broadcasting directives to its followers and agents below the 17th Parallel. This aggressive objective was frankly confirmed by a Congress of the Lao Dong (Communist) Party in Hanoi in September 1960. Their "momentous task," the delegates were instructed, was to "liberate" the south, and North Vietnam accordingly was being "transformed into a firm base for the struggle of national reunification." Three months later the manifesto announcing formation of the National Liberation Front used the identical language and slogans of the Hanoi Congress.

It was then that the activated underground began the rapid enlargement of its terrorist operations. In June 1962 the International Commission issued a majority report attesting that arms, munitions and other supplies were flowing from the north into the south. The victims of Viet Cong massacres, counted in hundreds in the first post-Geneva years, now rose to thousands.

The pretense that it was a "civil war" was believed only by political innocents. The conflict was launched and managed by the Hanoi leadership across an international frontier. The extent to which the aggressors then rallied or coerced support within the nation under attack did not cancel out the facts of the north's initiative, control, and responsibility.

The attack on South Vietnam followed a course strictly in line with the classic Mao Tse-tung strategy for "wars of liberation"—phased, that is, from subversion, terror, and guerrilla operations to a climax in conventional warfare. Except that the invasion was not sudden and overt, but gradual and expanded over a period of years, it was as much a foreign aggression as the communist assault on South Korea.

Several times in earlier centuries the Vietnamese had been split into two nations by the exigencies of conquest and resistance. Now they were again divided, by a piece of paper in Geneva. Despite the growing depredations of the Viet Cong, the South Vietnamese were grateful for a few brief years of comparative peace. Their numbers now expanded by nearly a million fugitives from communism from above the 17th Parallel, they returned to their fields and shops.

Such is the background of this militant people, both our allies and adversaries in Vietnam. There is nothing wrong with their fighting qualities on either side.

My own tasks in Vietnam included the responsibility of being senior U.S. advisor to the Army of the Republic of Vietnam in their First Corps area—a force of seventy thousand officers and men, from Popular Force platoons to regular infantry divisions. My knowledge of these men is a product of two years of association with them, both in training and on the battle-field.

As a professional soldier I recognize and respect them as superb light infantry. They lack our heavy weapons, our technical skill at using all our vast resources, our enormously expensive but vital air mobility. On the other hand, they are brilliant improvisers, they can move by foot over ground we consider nearly impassable, subsist on only a portion of what we would consider a normal day's ration of water, food, and ammunition, and fight like devils at the end of a grueling march.

The Regional and Popular forces (RF and PF) have a peculiar élan of their own, in spite of obsolete weapons, cast-off uniforms, and dangerous, lonely assignments. They have a sense of purpose, pride, and an exceptional skill for their segment of the war, that difficult hinterland between cities and towns, in and among the villages and the people. What they need is support —powerful forces ready to come to their aid when their little, static, indispensable outposts are attacked in force. A network of support—ours or that of the Army of the Republic of Vietnam—so no man stands alone.

It is illogical to make direct comparisons between American and Vietnamese units, and even more senseless to make them between the Army of the Republic of Vietnam and the Viet Cong. The Vietnamese soldier is not on a year's tour of duty in Vietnam; unless he is killed or disabled his war seldom lasts less than five years and may last his lifetime. His officers are men who learn their trade in the rude practicalities of battle; no product of command and staff schools or National War Colleges, they are lucky to have had eight years of schooling and to be able to read and write. Still, they can command their own units and do it well.

When someone asks me, "Why don't the Vietnamese fight?" I often think—and sometimes tell my questioner—of one hot day

Doc-Lap!

in Quang Ngai Province when one of my own battalions was in heavy contact with a Viet Cong Main Force regiment, machine-gun fire raking their positions, unable to move, and only one Vietnamese Army battalion anywhere close enough to help. My Vietnamese counterpart, General Thi, had flown with me to the area and saw, as I did, how critical the situation was. He gave quick orders to move his battalion to the aid of my Marines. For them to close with the enemy position meant moving across several hundred yards of open rice fields. We saw the battalion arrive and watched as they unhesitatingly moved across the open area; watched as the Viet Cong machine guns shifted to fire on them; watched as the little men charged on, dropping yet continuing to move, watched them overrun the machine-gun positions, assaulting right into the flaming muzzles.

They saved a lot of my Marines that day, with their own bodies, for fully half the battalion littered that open field, some moving slightly, some very still—the way it has to be done sometimes; the way we had to cross the airfield on Peleliu in 1944 or seize Suribachi in 1945. The hard way. And people still ask me, "Why don't the Vietnamese fight?"

Too often an invidious comparison is made between the Viet Cong and the Army of the Republic of Vietnam, as if only the Viet Cong are brave, cunning, and efficient. Too often even we who fight them see them in distortion, since we meet only the brave and feel only the sting of their fire.

There was a little outpost near Danang and it was hit one night—a sudden attack out of the darkness, rockets and machine-gun fire, followed by an infantry assault with demolitions. It was a hard, hot fight and we took many casualties. Suddenly it was over. The outpost had held and the echoes of the firing were dying in the distant hills. An airplane dropped a flare and in its brilliant light we saw the backs of our enemy. There was just a handful of them left.

Doc-Lap!

They were using the big wicker panniers from peasant homes to drag their wounded behind them; they had thrust meathooks into the bodies of their dead and were pulling them across the paddies, breasting the mud, struggling down to a small river and escape, leaving glistening trails behind them like worms crawling out of a flashlight's glare. And all their terrible suffering, their loss, their defeat, was limned in the cold white light.

These were the agonies that caused eleven thousand of them to give up in 1965, surrendering to us and to the Army of the Republic of Vietnam; caused twenty thousand of them to surrender in 1966, twenty-seven thousand in 1967, and another forty-seven thousand in 1969. Agonies and disillusionment, for this proud, patient people will fight for freedom from oppression, not against it. It is for them to decide who are the oppressors, who is for or against independence—*Doc-Lap*. And then the answer to the war will come from the people themselves, down at the rice roots of the country.

9

Rice-Roots Support

Of all our innovations in Vietnam none was as successful, as lasting in effect, or as useful for the future as the Combined Action Program.

Like many good ideas, the system was basically simple: Help the local defense forces at the hamlet level with training, equipment, support, and the actual presence of American fighting men. As with many good ideas, there are those who would assume credit not due them. I can unequivocally state that the original suggestion was made by Capt. John J. Mullin, Jr., the first plans made by Maj. Cullen B. Zimmerman, with the approval of the Commanding Officer of the 3d Battalion, 4th Marines (Regiment), Lt. Col. William W. Taylor. The first Combined Action Unit was commanded by First Lt. Paul Ek and commenced operations on August 3, 1965. The results were far beyond our most optimistic hopes.

The local Popular Force soldier—the hamlet and village guard—was the poorest equipped, least trained, and most inadequately supported of all the government forces in the Republic of Vietnam, yet none was more important to the security of the people. He had a signal advantage over all others: he was defending his own home, family, and neighbors. The Popular Force soldier knew every person in his community by face and name; he knew each paddyfield, trail, bush, or bamboo clump, each family shelter, tunnel, and buried rice urn. He knew in most cases the local Viet Cong guerrilla band, and it was not uncommon for him to be related to one or more of them by blood or other family ties.

The basic village force was one Popular Force platoon—about thirty men—divided into three ragtag squads. By happy coincidence the Marine Corps rifle squad is unique in that it is composed of three "fire teams," each with a corporal as leader and three riflemen, all of them under a sergeant squad leader.

By the summer of 1965 the Marines had worked with the Popular Force units many times and found them extremely useful, with intimate knowledge of their local area and of enemy operations in it. It occurred to Captain Mullin one day that one Marine rifle squad would provide a seasoned sergeant to work constantly with a Popular Force platoon leader, and a fire team to work directly with each Popular Force squad. If a Marine squad could be spared to live in the village with the Popular Force platoon, not only would there be a day and night force of considerable combined strength but also an exchange of knowledge that would benefit both components. There were also dangers: How loyal were the Popular Force soldiers? Were they government soldiers by day and Viet Cong at night? Would they defect in a fight and leave the Marine squad to its own resources? We had to learn.

Captain Mullin took one Marine platoon, a lieutenant, and three rifle squads, and made a test. Near Hué he selected three villages, each with a Popular Force platoon as a local guard force, in an area where the Viet Cong were known to be active. The Vietnamese officials were cooperative, and in a week the first three Combined Action Units were in operation. The results were beyond expectations. The Marines adapted quickly to their new role; the Popular Force platoons were delighted.

Rice-Roots Support

Here, in each of their villages, was a team of highly trained regulars, and all the resources of the Americans to come to their aid in the event of trouble. No longer did they feel alone. Their appearance smartened, their morale soared, their efficiency increased. And when it came to a fight, they now fought, for the odds were no longer hopeless.

Needing every success, we had found one. Once the system had proved itself, I went to the Commander of the 1st Vietnamese Division, General Chuan. He too immediately recognized its worth. Together we expanded the Combined Action Unit program: he directed the Popular Forces to initiate the new units, I provided seasoned squads of Marines to the selected villages. By the end of 1965 these units were saturating wide areas of the densely populated lowlands with thousands of patrols and ambushes, day and night watches—and the Viet Cong were being hit where it hurt them most.

The village of Binh Nghia was typical. A cluster of five hamlets, Binh Nghia contained about five thousand people. It was "guarded" by a Popular Force platoon of twenty-eight men. There were two companies of Viet Cong generally operating in the area from nearby mountain and jungle camps. The Popular Force unit was frightened. The Viet Cong moved in and out of the village at will during the night, taking money from the villagers, conscripting new men, confiscating rice. Only the day belonged to the legitimate government. Into this unhappy situation came a squad of Marines led by Sgt. Joseph Sullivan, of Cincinnati, Ohio.

As they had been instructed, Sergeant Sullivan and his men lived no better and no worse than the Popular Force platoon. Theirs was no world of PXs, movies, and cold beer, but of tension and constant danger. Sullivan and his men went to work in their own way. They began to patrol at night outside the village and stand watches with the Popular Force troops through the long, dark hours. During the day, instead of sleeping, they taught the Popular Force troopers the proper use of weapons, how to fight as a team, how the little Marine squad was backed up by artillery and aircraft and many more troops if necessary.

Soon the Popular Force men were accompanying the Marines on their patrols and ambushes outside the village in the soft tropical night, and as they gained confidence they began their own night patrols. The Viet Cong knew what was going on—there were more than a hundred families in the village with some ties to the guerrillas in the hills.

There were probes against the new, active defense of the village and clashes in the night that showed it no longer belonged to the Viet Cong by default. The people of Binh Nghia began to respect their little local soldiers more, and they began to show their natural warmth toward the Marines as well, instead of fearful restraint under the all-seeing eyes of the Viet Cong and their sympathizers. Information welled up from the people—information on the goings and comings of the Viet Cong, their food and arms caches, their local hiding places. Sergeant Sullivan and his men grew thinner, and the fatigue lines on their young faces deepened, as the prosperity, health, and well-being of the villagers improved. They were winning this war at the rice-roots level, and they knew it. So did the Viet Cong.

Those desperate men in the rain forest could not afford to lose, and, in keeping with their philosophy, would sooner destroy their people than suffer defeat in controlling them. They came down out of the mountains one dark night and made a battlefield of the village. Together the Marines and Popular Force soldiers fought them off. By dawn the Viet Cong had withdrawn, dragging their dead and wounded with them, and Sgt. Joseph Sullivan, U.S. Marine Corps, had given his life for the people of Binh Nghia; so had Mr. Phoc, the Popular Force platoon commander, a son of the village for which he died.

Rice-Roots Support

The Viet Cong struck again the next night, and one last time on the next; the force that Sergeant Sullivan and Mr. Phoc had built closed ranks and threw them back each time. When it was over, the Viet Cong had been decimated and Binh Nghia was a free community.

There are now more than a hundred such communities—not all with freedom so hard won as Binh Nghia's, but each based upon the dynamic formula of Marines combined with Popular Force units as the basic security force. These miniature melting pots have held against major Viet Cong assaults, infiltration, subversion, propaganda, threat, coercion, and every other weapon available to the enemy. The Marines involved have had "Wanted, Dead or Alive" prices of 10,000 piasters placed on them by the Viet Cong; they endure sniping, booby traps, mines, and ambush. The Vietnamese leaders with whom they work are subjected to assassination attempts and reprisals against their families.

As these men of both nations fight they work, and their villages are marked by clinics and schools, clean market places, roads, bridges, and pure water. The Marines learn the language of the people and at the same time teach the people English. They wear the blue-bordered red scarf of the Popular Forces, eat the food of the people once each day and share their own food with them. It is grueling, sensitive, endless effort, and it has its own rewards. Many of the Marines in the Combined Action Units volunteer to extend their time in Vietnam to finish what they have begun. Many have continued their association with their village long after returning home, and their presence is maintained by packages mailed to "their" people of the village. Some even find themselves homesick for the gentle, pleasant people they have left behind in Vietnam—the people they helped to smile again after years of oppression and want.

Rice-Roots Support

What is more significant is that equivalent sentiments arise among the villagers. Mostly we know this from the men who live and work with them, for those of us who are only occasional visitors are met with the polite reserve accorded strangers. Once in a while, however, the real feeling shows through and we outsiders catch a glimpse of what our men in the villages know so well.

One morning I arrived at my office near Danang and saw a young Vietnamese girl in the outer room. When I asked the clerk why she was there at such an early hour, he told me she had come to return a watch lost by a Marine. She was only about eleven, shy and pretty, and it took a little coaxing to get her to talk, but when she did, it was in good English. I asked her why she had returned the watch. She showed it to me—an expensive gold wristwatch with a Marine's name engraved on the back—and explained that she could not sell or keep it because it belonged to a Marine and she liked Marines.

I asked her why she liked Marines. She replied, "My father was a corporal in the Vietnamese Marine Corps. He was killed by the Viet Cong two years ago. I like American Marines because they came to my village and drove the Viet Cong away. They made my village a safe place to live. They helped us rebuild our school and church and market place."

When I asked her how she learned to speak English so well, she told me, "My brother taught me. My mother had money to send only one of us to school, so she sent my oldest brother. Each evening my brother comes home from the school and teaches me and my other two brothers and sisters what he has learned that day."

I thought of the watch, glistening on the table, equivalent to perhaps a year's income to this struggling family, and of the dignity and pride and sincere affection represented by its return. I rewarded her with some Vietnamese piasters—not so many that she would be insulted, not so few that it would be no help—and she thanked me with a charming curtsy as she left. Alone in the office for a moment, before beginning the tasks of the new day, I felt the warmth of reassurance that the sacrifices of our own people were not in vain, that they were not made without the deep appreciation and everlasting thanks of such Vietnamese as that little girl, a child of eleven, raised in a country hamlet where for so many years poverty, disease, war, and hopelessness had dominated her environment. She had just clearly demonstrated traits of character that surmounted these handicaps, traits learned from the adults who had raised her, the villagers with whom she had been associated during her few years, men and women of good will, dignity, and pride. These were the people who could and should inherit the future of Vietnam; who deserved our help, not sneers or abandonment.

There was another time, when Huynh Ba Trinh, the village chief of Hoa Long, spoke out. His arm was in a cast, shattered by a Viet Cong grenade. His wife and two of his children were nursing wounds from the same attack. Huynh Ba Trinh is a proud, stubborn man who knows his people and refuses to give up his village to the communists. He spoke heatedly and from the heart: "My people are very poor. Only a few of them went to school. They did not understand the Viet Cong in the first years. They believed what the Viet Cong said. After nine years of living with the Viet Cong they can now understand. The people do not want the Viet Cong. They fear them and hate them. The villagers have learned that what the Viet Cong say is from the mouth alone; it is not from the heart. The people know that the Americans have come to help them. The Marines have not taken rice from the people. They do not take farm tools. They do not murder and torture. They do not take money. They do not take hostages."

A Popular Force private said it differently and at less length, but also from the heart. Watching the bandaged Americans being carried to the waiting helicopter, he shifted the big rifle on his thin shoulder, murmured, "The Marines give many bloods to my country," and trudged off to his assigned position, a small, dusty, firm figure.

These individual feelings, like drops of rain in the mountains, grew into freshets and began to flood the coastal plain. Each was a little battle won, a defeat to the Viet Cong. For a year the communists watched their ranks thin as the people turned more and more toward us and their own government. Increasingly, we became the fish swimming in the sea of people, with the guerrilla flopping on the bank, gasping for air.

We had found the key to our main problem—how to fight the war. The struggle was in the rice paddies, in and among the people, not passing through, but living among them, night and day, sharing their victories and defeats, suffering with them if need be, and joining with them in steps toward a better life long overdue. The Combined Action Units were a major part of this; so was our Civic Action Program, the efforts of our own civilians from the State Department and AID and the USIA, and the men and women of voluntary agencies working throughout Vietnam—along with the workers of the government of Vietnam.

Then, suddenly, came a terrible blow—not on the military but on the political front.

General Lewis W. Walt in Vietnam. He received his fourth star in 1969 and is at present Assistant Commandant, U.S. Marine Corps.

Villagers fleeing their ancestral home to escape Viet Cong terror.

Travel for the South Vietnamese involved the danger of mined roads, snipers, and ambush.

"Golden Fleece"—U.S. Marine and native guards protect the
harvesters of rice.

Primitive Montagnards in their hill hamlet after a Viet Cong raid.

"It was hard, dirty fighting. . . ."
Right: A Marine patrol hunting the enemy. *Below:* Machine gunners, a breed unto themselves.

Below: Much of the struggle is in the rice paddies.

"One of them small, limping, and hopeful; one of them big, powerful, cautious, and puzzled, like the two nations they represented."

"Many were ill and we gave them care. . . . Many were almost naked and we clothed them."

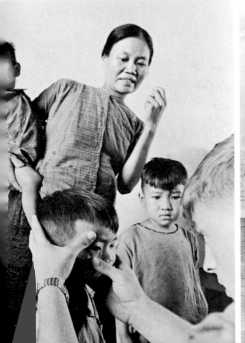

General Walt makes some new friends.   Popular Force fought with Marines.

Combined Action Unit
—Marine rifle squad
lives, works, and fights
in the village. "By the
end of 1965, these units
were saturating wide
areas of densely popu-
lated lowlands with
thousands of patrols
and ambushes, day and
night watches—and the
Viet Cong were being
hit where it hurt them
most."

Above: Republic of South Vietnam raising their flag at a hillside outpost. *Below:* "The Viet Cong were firing back now, from the shelter of trees only yards away."

The enemy: with rare exceptions the Viet Cong is a very young
man—as young as fourteen in this case

10

Political
Crisis: I

Our first year in Vietnam was a hard one, but it was far worse
on the Viet Cong. From a situation just short of triumph, they
had been blocked, beaten, and thrown back into the hills or
forced underground again. The young government they had
almost extinguished had survived with our help. The Viet Cong
sources of food, recruits, and intelligence in the densely populated and intensively cultivated lowlands had been progressively denied them. They seemed still to be in a state of shock
over the massive infusion of American combat power, matériel,
and moral support into the conflict. Instead of adapting to this
new circumstance, they had continued to fight the war as they
had against the South Vietnamese, and neither their military
defeats nor the evidence of their deteriorated control over the
people had any noticeable effect on this inflexibility.

As 1966 began and the first anniversary of our original landings approached, we were already planning to link up the expanding areas of control from Hué, Danang, and Chu Lai, putting the bulk of the population and agriculture and all of the
key roads and railroads in our area within a protecting enve-
lope in which the freedom of choice was up to the individual
Vietnamese—without a gun at his temple.

Political Crisis: I

Then, swiftly and unexpectedly, our hopes were collapsed. Not by the Viet Cong, but even more tragically by our friends and allies, the South Vietnamese themselves.

On March 10, 1966, Nguyen Chanh Thi, the Vietnamese Corps Commander in our area, was relieved of his command by Premier Nguyen Cao Ky and the government in Saigon. In our own system, such an action might have been looked upon with regret, but hardly would have been cataclysmic to the prosecution of the war or to the political structure of the government. But this was not our system.

Under the conditions of war emergency the corps commanders in Vietnam held both political and military power. There were only four such commanders in the entire country. They acted with almost total authority in their own regions, while enormously influencing the actions of the central government in Saigon. Perhaps the most independent of all these was the Commander of the I Corps region, geographically farthest from Saigon and controlling two of the three largest cities in the country.

There were personal loyalties involved. The Vietnamese Air Force could be expected to act in the interests of the national government largely because Premier Ky was also the Chief of Staff of their service. The separate battalions of Vietnamese Marines and airborne units, used generally throughout the country but based in Saigon, could also be expected to identify with the central government. The Vietnamese Army at large, however, and particularly the regional and local "popular" forces, were as provincial as our Continental Army in 1776 or the Fourth Virginia Cavalry in 1861. Where the leadership was good—and that of the I Corps was exceptional—the loyalty to the commander was deep-rooted and sometimes paralleled that given the government.

In this situation, far more delicate and volatile than any of us had imagined, the relief of the I Corps commander triggered a series of events that almost tore the country apart. In only a few days most of what we had accomplished in almost a year appeared to collapse. The American forces found themselves nearly alone in trying to maintain some semblance of order in a hopelessly complex situation.

Within twenty-four hours of the Vietnamese commander's relief by Saigon thousands of demonstrators were trooping the streets of Danang, voicing their disagreement with the government and demanding his reinstatement. The mayor tried to resign and his resignation was refused. An organization called "The Military-Civilian Struggle Committee" was formed and expressed its support of the dismissed general and its opposition to the Saigon government.

The next day the movement spread, with ominous signs of a schism within the Vietnamese military. The Danang radio was taken over by the dissidents and began broadcasts against the central government. More rallies and demonstrations racked Danang. The university students at Hué joined the "Struggle" movement. Most ominous of all, the Military-Civilian Struggle Committee began to claim control of the armed forces of Quang Nam Province—the Vietnamese state that included Danang and the most vital military installations of the area: the airfield at Danang, the port facilities, and most of the major supply areas. A general strike was called, crippling the unloading of ships, military construction, and many other support activities essential to our operations.

At this time the Struggle Movement, at least on the surface, was anticommunist and pro-ally. The deposed General Thi, whom they were supporting, consistently called for order and discipline among his followers. There were no incidents involving Americans. Except for the general strike, which lasted only a few days, cooperation continued between ourselves and the Vietnamese.

The issues involved were resentment at the peremptory relief of a respected and popular leader, the regional dissatisfaction of being dictated to by Saigon, and the common complaints of corruption and inefficiency in the young central government. Undoubtedly there was also political opportunism. The Struggle Movement appeared to be something more than spontaneous. It was well organized, moved quickly into the situation, and conducted its operations with some skill. However, it operated as a newcomer among vigorous and entrenched competitors: those loyal to the Saigon government, established political parties opposed to Saigon rule, the Vietnamese Catholics, who generally acted in concert politically, and the Buddhists.

The Buddhists, as a political group, entered the scene on March 19 with a rally at Danang, also objecting to the relief of the original Corps Commander and vilifying the Saigon government. This was alarming. Vietnam is a predominantly Buddhist country. The sects are a potent political force as well as a religious institution, seeking both power and privilege on a national scale. Within a day their bid for popular support spread to Hué, with the young university students drawn in as activists. The Hué radio station was seized by a group of these students and the civilian airwaves were now filled with protests and denunciation of the central government, from the Struggle Movement in Danang and the Buddhists in Hué.

So far the Americans had stayed out of the mainstream of events, watching, waiting, reluctant to enter an internal political fight. The Viet Cong seemed as shocked and surprised as we. Military operations dwindled on both sides as the internal paroxysm developed. But we knew there was opportunity here for the Viet Cong, and it soon became evident.

The first indication was a call for force—leaflets strewn in the streets of Danang demanded that the issue be decided by bullets. The same day the Struggle Movement was renamed the *Luc-Luong nhan-dan tranh-thu cach-mang*—the "Popular

Political Crisis: I

Forces to Struggle for the Revolution." In the weird world of doctrinaire communism such a title is necessary; to us and to the pro-Saigon elements it was a danger signal of likely Viet Cong infiltration of the opposition movements.

Rapidly the original issue—the deposing of a locally popular figure—faded imto the background. The Buddhist-student movement centered in Hué became more significant. Anti-communist and pro-ally statements disappeared; anti-government pronouncements bccame more virulent, and vilification of the Americans began to appear, including English-language banners intended to provoke incidents from our own men. Activists were ready to inflame any incident—a minor traffic accident or any thoughtless act on the part of an American—into a riot. It was a tense period demanding enormous restraint.

Our Marine Corps forces were largely in the field. Construction, the landing and transportation of supplies, and activities in and around Hué and Danang were suspended. The Vietnamese armed forces in our area were standing by, inactive and confused.

By April the situation had become severe. The original Struggle Movement was in the hands of the students. Most of the I Corps area, including Hué and Danang, was operating independently of the central government. It was as if California, with Los Angeles and San Francisco, had seceded from the United States. The civilian radio stations seized by the dissidents poured out a torrent of anti-government and anti-American propaganda. The Vietnamese armed forces were torn with divided loyalties—to the government, to the deposed general, to the people of the region, to the Buddhists, to their own unit, in accordance with the political complexion of their commanders. Action by the central government was expected at any time, and no one knew what the result would be.

I had to sort out my own position in this chaos. Events were developing too rapidly and too locally for anyone else to make an effective judgment. I talked with my best and most experienced confidants, men who had seen wars and revolutions in other places—including my political advisor from the State Department, Sam Thomsen, as fine a professional as I have ever met. In him we had a man who spoke the language of the people fluently and knew them intimately; one who could advise us with sagacity and skill and keep his head in a tight moment. Together, we came to these conclusions:

1. My responsibility toward the lives of Americans, and the American-built or -maintained installations in our areas, was clear. A threat to them, from whatever faction, could not be countenanced.

2. My responsibility to the people of Vietnam obligated me to prevent an armed confrontation between opposing factions if that was in my power.

I didn't have long to wait before these principles were put to the test. On April 3 the Vietnamese government declared Danang to be in the hands of those sympathetic to the Viet Cong. The next day two Vietnamese Marine Corps battalions arrived by air from Saigon. The critical move had been made. At the same time, Vietnamese Army units, proclaiming general support of the Struggle Movement, began moving toward Danang and Hué.

I exerted every influence I had to convince the troops from Saigon to stay within the confines of the airbase at Danang, to give us some control over an open clash between South Vietnamese armed units. Fortunately, there was a bond already between us as fellow Marines, and they were willing to listen. As a precaution against what might happen, I began to evacuate American citizens from the cities and recalled the American advisors attached to the dissident Vietnamese Army units.

Hour by hour we watched the situation degenerate. The students in Hué demanded and began to receive arms, organizing into a student militia to fight on the side of their segment of the

Struggle Movement. Government coffers of money and food were released to the Struggle Movement leaders, and it began to look even more as if we had a civil war on our hands. By every means possible we kept informed of troop movements and events, remaining aloof, but watching for the moment when it might become our direct problem as well as one involving the Vietnamese.

The crisis came on April 9, directly involving the United States forces for the first time. On that day we learned that a powerful military force was advancing on Danang from the south.

The Danang airbase was the major military installation in our area. United States troops—Air Force, Marine, and Army —operated from it. American and Vietnamese civil aircraft landed and took off from its confines. The Vietnamese Air Force, solidly loyal to Premier Ky and the government of Vietnam, controlled it and used it as their own primary airbase in the northern part of the country. A huge complex, any attack on that base to cripple or destroy the Vietnamese Air Force there, or any attack on the troop units from Saigon that now occupied it, not only would involve American forces, but without question would also threaten the lives and safety of American men and the destruction of American property essential to our operations.

Now a sizable armed force with armored vehicles and four pieces of medium artillery was advancing on that base, commanded by a Vietnamese Army officer I knew well, Colonel Yeu, with the expressed intention of supporting the Struggle Movement. I thought of six-inch artillery shells crashing into the American aircraft, barracks, ammunition, and fuel that crowded the base area; of Vietnamese soldiers fighting Vietnamese Marines and airmen—and the Viet Cong waiting to move in and pick up the pieces.

As the column moved north toward Danang, a flight of Vietnamese Air Force attack planes took off, loaded with armament. I called their headquarters and asked them to return to base, knowing that when they did I had also assumed the responsibility to prevent the threatened battle. They buzzed the approaching troops a time or two and returned without attacking—and the column continued its movement. As they came within range of the airfield with their four big guns, I knew I had to stop them and I sent one man to do it.

Col. John Chaisson was my operations officer and one of the most brilliant and courageous men I knew. With an interpreter, he boarded a helicopter and flew down to the advancing column, momentarily stopped at a small river, and landed deliberately in the face of the threatening artillery pieces.

The Vietnamese colonel was there. Chaisson made the first overture: Could the two of them, he asked, meet with me at my headquarters and discuss the situation? As expected, the Vietnamese refused. Chaisson presented my position: the colonel's unit represented a threat to the Danang airbase protected by Americans at the request of the Vietnamese government; it was also a threat to American lives and property for which we were responsible to our own government; therefore, we could not permit him to advance any further.

Chaisson hoped he was believed, for we were not bluffing. We had prevented the Vietnamese Air Force attack, but we were prepared to do the same—and more—ourselves if it came to a fight. A flight of Marine jet fighter-bombers was circling overhead. We had Marine artillery trained on the position. A Marine infantry unit was inconspicuously nearby, with direct-fire cannon leveled at the Vietnamese artillery pieces. Sooner than have those six-inch guns hurling high explosives into the airbase, we would have opened fire on them ourselves and taken the consequences. It was a tense and tragic moment.

Colonel Yeu replied, with deep emotion: he was a friend of the Marines and of General Walt, but he had come to fight the

Political Crisis: I

Saigon government troops who threatened the local people; he had come to lay down his own life if necessary, and if it were at the hands of his friend General Walt or those of the Saigon government, it made no difference.

It was nearly noon on a bright, hot day. The sun glistened on the wings of the circling jets and oiled muzzles of the Vietnamese artillery as the two colonels talked. Hundreds of men, their weapons loaded, looked across at other men who had been allies the day before and wondered what the war had come to. The Vietnamese artillerymen began to uncase the big shells, as they had been taught to do by their American advisors, and then to insert the fuses, ready for firing.

Chaisson was an artilleryman himself. He had been one before some of these men were born, when the Marines were still using French 75s from World War I, and he knew that the time for talking was over. Pointing to the guns and the uncased, fused ammunition, he demanded their withdrawal, stating our position once again: we could not tolerate the threat to the Danang airbase; if any further advance were made or if a move were made to fire, it would become necessary to annihilate the unit. This said, Chaisson turned and walked away to his waiting helicopter, punctuating his last words with a swirl of dust and roar of engine, leaving the next move to the Vietnamese.

Carefully we watched. The moment of high drama passed. There was a pause of inactivity; then, leisurely, the threatening guns went out of firing position, and although they did not leave, neither did they advance. It was a decent compromise between two determined men, without embarrassment to either, and the airbase stayed unharmed. The next day the government of Vietnam also relieved the newly appointed commander of I Corps, and no one cared at all. It was quiet for a few days. The Danang radio went back into government hands and began to broadcast soothing messages. The Hué radio also went back to government broadcasts, with the rather curious compromise of permitting the Struggle Movement two hours each day for anti-government broadcasts. The Vietnamese Marines who had kept their faith with me and remained at the airbase throughout returned again to Saigon, and the Vietnamese Army in our area resumed operations against the Viet Cong—to the relief of thousands of American Marines who had been carrying the whole load of the war for more than a month. General Thi, whose relief from command had started the whole affair, publicly disclaimed any sympathy with the Struggle Movement or any aspirations to high office.

Beneath the new calm, however, strong undercurrents still flowed. The Buddhists had now become foremost in the complicated interplay of forces and were carefully solidifying their position, concentrating on control of the Vietnamese Army units in the area and duplicating their command structure with one of their own. On May 15 the crisis flared again.

It was a quiet Sunday morning, and promised to be a quiet day. There had been little or no activity involving the Struggle Movement for several days, and all appeared to be returning to normal. In fact, in an effort to emphasize the return to normality, the new Vietnamese commander had planned a social affair that evening and invited me to attend. This new confidence was smashed by the roar of a massive airlift into Danang, beginning just at dawn—Vietnamese Marines again, followed by airborne battalions loyal to the Saigon government, landing and debarking from civil and military Vietnamese aircraft.

No time here for exerting influence, for compromise or negotiation. As they debarked the troops thrust directly into the city of Danang, seizing the Vietnamese Army headquarters there. With the planes still landing and taking off, the new Corps commander came dashing to me by jeep, pursued by Vietnamese tanks. He asked sanctuary. I put him in my own quarters and promised him safety.

Political Crisis: I

The senior military officer in Vietnam, General Vien, Chairman of their Joint General Staff, arrived in Danang, followed soon after by Premier Ky himself. Somewhat frantically, we used every possible resource to find out what was going on. Reports flooded in: the Saigon troops had seized the Danang radio station, the City Hall, and other key buildings and public utilities; local Vietnamese Army units were on the move toward Danang from the south, and more were heading toward Danang from Hué; the Vietnamese Air Force was attacking Vietnamese Army units outside of Danang. The Chairman of the Joint Chiefs of Staff in Washington, General Earl Wheeler, called to find out what was happening, as did the Secretary of State, Dean Rusk.

I went to the Vietnamese commanding general, now in my quarters guarded by several husky Marines, and asked if he could stop the movements of his own troops heading toward Danang. He said he would try but could promise nothing. I requested that the Vietnamese Air Force not attack the Vietnamese troops. They agreed. I tried to contact the Premier but found he had returned to Saigon with the Chairman of the Joint General Staff. Helplessly we waited out the night, counting what blessings remained: American troops were not yet involved; the shooting had died down; the Viet Cong were quiet.

The next morning I was notified that the general in my quarters was being relieved of his command and a new one would be designated as the Commanding General of I Corps. He arrived from Saigon the following day, and we provided him with a helicopter and escort to visit the two divisions of his new command. Sensing trouble, I asked one of my most senior and able officers to undertake the task. Brig. Gen. Jonas M. Platt was a tall, experienced, and very capable officer I had known for many years. I had a feeling he would be needed.

They took off first for Hué—General Platt, the Vietnamese

[123]

general and his aide, a senior U.S. Army advisor, and a Vietnamese photographer. They used the Army advisor's helicopter. The visit was a strange one. There was the usual honor guard, introductions, a briefing, and honors again on departure, but all the senior officers of the division were conspicuously absent. As our party was boarding the helicopter to depart an unruly crowd of civilians and a few soldiers broke into the compound, unrestrained by the guards, and began milling dangerously around the helicopter and its rotating blades. From the crowd a Vietnamese Army lieutenant pulled out his .45-caliber pistol and started firing at the helicopter at close range. As the second bullet went ricocheting into the cabin, the Army gunner at the door of the aircraft turned his machine gun on the lieutenant and cut him down with a single burst.

Blades whirling, the helicopter took off to safety, the honor guard standing at attention as their commanding general departed. Thereafter he commanded from the safety of my headquarters until, like his predecessors, he was relieved of command.

II

Political
Crisis: II

In Danang a new problem had arisen. East of the main city, across a river, was a flat, unarable, and thinly populated area connected to Danang itself by a long patched bridge. It was the kind of place you could use for lumber yards, or fuel or ammunition dumps, easy to guard and disturbing nothing but the sand fleas.

When the Vietnamese Marines took over Danang, they stopped at the west end of the bridge. Across the river the Vietnamese Army had a number of supply facilities similar to our own, generally in the hands of one of their engineer units. These troops, part of the I Corps, had been associated with the Struggle Movement in an inactive sense, but the river made a convenient dividing line between them and the government troops.

The Vietnamese Marines had moved across the bridge at one time, and set up positions just a few hundred yards from the engineer unit on the east end, but were pulled back to their own side at my request. To prevent a recurrence of the incident, and with the concurrence of the Vietnamese Corps Commander, I had put a Marine unit at the west end of the bridge to act as a buffer. The bridge was important to all of us, as the connection between the mainland and the extensive supply facilities dotted around the scrub and palmetto of what we called Danang East. It was therefore a serious matter when my Marines near that bridge informed me that the Vietnamese Army engineers on the other side had installed enough explosives to blow out their half of the bridge whenever they wished.

I called on Colonel Chaisson again to try and sort it out, covering him with a Marine platoon of infantry hastily brought up from the south to get some of our own people on the east end of the bridge. Chaisson, rapidly becoming an expert on confrontations, got there first and began discussions with the Vietnamese engineer commander and his U.S. Army advisor. It turned out that the engineers had not only mined the bridge, but had also prepared demolition charges in a nearby ammunition dump containing six thousand tons of ammunition. Their American advisor was furious but helpless.

As they talked the leading squad of the U.S. Marine platoon arrived, commanded by a very large, very competent black sergeant. As they came into sight hurried orders were given in Vietnamese, and the engineer unit deployed into battle positions facing the oncoming Marines. Two heavy machine guns covering the bridge were switched and pointed at the Marines. A Vietnamese warrant officer and a couple of his engineers moved to the detonator, conspicuously placed out toward the center of the bridge. Someone on the Vietnamese side fired twice at the Marines, and they too deployed and dove to the ground, ready to fight; but under the iron control of their sergeant they held their fire. Chaisson silently blessed all coolheaded sergeants: one had just saved a bridge and a lot of lives.

It was still a very tense situation. The U.S. Army advisor had reached the end of his own patience and swung his jeep in front of the muzzles of the two machine guns. Chaisson somehow had to get the Marines into position at the bridge. His solution was brusque but effective. Putting a big arm about the slim shoulders of a Vietnamese officer, he practically moved him physically out into the open, between the Marines and the Vietnamese engineers. From some distance it was a picture of friendly solidarity. Keeping a solid grip on the Vietnamese, Chaisson motioned the Marines up and told the big, calm squad leader to mingle with the Vietnamese, be friendly, but keep an eye on the detonator. This done, Chaisson got back to my command post to let me know what was going on.

We had made headway on the problem, but it wasn't enough. As long as that bridge was wired for demolition, we were at the mercy of whoever held the plunger. Colonel Chaisson and I drove down to the bridge, arriving at the west end of the Danang side.

My patience with uncompromising and occasionally arrogant Struggle Movement commanders was wearing very thin. We held a brief council at our end of the bridge: Chaisson, myself, several of my other officers, and the engineer officer who was American advisor to the troublesome unit at the other end who told us there was enough high explosive set in to destroy the bridge. He thought he knew the rigging of the charges well enough to be able to cut or disconnect the wiring between the detonator and the explosives, but the attention of the Vietnamese would have to be distracted enough to permit him to clamber beneath the bridge, then find and follow the electric wires unnoticed.

I was the senior in rank, the biggest in stature, and probably the angriest of the group—a combination that made me the most likely distractor. I told the engineer I would meet with the Vietnamese commander at the center of the bridge, that I wanted the explosives disarmed while we talked, and that I wanted to know when they were safe. Signaling for an inter-preter to come along, I started out on the bridge.

The Struggle Force commander on the opposite side—a

short, slight warrant officer—came out to meet me. We met about midway. He was very formal, very curt, and spoke only Vietnamese. Through the interpreter I told him my purpose: to prevent destruction of the bridge because it was vital to his own people. I assured him that in keeping with this intent, I would guard the bridge with my own Marines and keep it intact until the internal troubles of the Vietnamese forces were resolved. The warrant officer was totally unreceptive. He told me he would not move his troops from the bridge. Looking me straight in the eye and speaking with firm conviction, he added that if I tried force he would have the bridge blown up on the spot—those were his orders, and he was prepared to carry them out.

Playing for time as well as trying to find some kind of reasonable solution, I asked whose orders these were. The minutes ticked by as I tried to get him to bring his commanding officer into the scene. Meanwhile, the Army engineer and a couple of Marines were moving among the trusses beneath us, locating and cutting lead-in wires. Finally, I spotted the sweat-soaked engineer officer, who gave me a silent thumbs-up signal. I hoped he had done his hurried job well.

Cutting the palaver short, I told my opponent he had five minutes to remove his troops and disconnect the detonator. He flatly refused—he had his orders and would carry them out. Repeatedly and pointedly I looked at my wristwatch and the second hand laboriously creeping around the dial.

Everything stood out vividly and unforgettably—the two machine guns at the far end of the bridge with ammunition belts of gleaming brass cartridges clinched into their receivers, manned by stolid, silent Vietnamese soldiers ready to open fire in our direction; the detonator, its plunger high, conspicuously out in clear view at the east end of the bridge, two Vietnamese engineers standing by it at the ready; the little officer straight and proud in front of me, determination and defiance obvious in his face. There was a heavily armed Marine Corps company behind me on the west bank, ready to cross at my signal. I had gone too far to back down. We would either take the bridge or die fighting for it. Anything less than that and we might as well go home and let the Bamboo Curtain slip down over another 17 million people.

The tedious progression of my watch finally reached the five-minute mark, and I signaled the Marines across, at the same time telling the warrant officer, "You leave me no choice but to force you and your troops off this bridge."

He glared at me, and suddenly in good English said, "General, we will die on this bridge together," raised his right arm, and swung it smartly to his side. I saw the plunger go down on the detonator at the far end of the bridge, and for one heartbeat wondered once again how well the engineer officer had done his work. Instead of an explosion I heard only the heavy tread of my Marines bearing down on us from the western side.

I turned to the warrant officer, not without pity. It is a shame to take such a moment away from a man. He seemed to shrivel there on the bridge. I gave him one last hard look, he who could have blown my hopes as well as a bridge with that dropping hand of his, yet a man I respected for his courage and will. Then I walked back across the bridge. My part in this was done.

We kept our own Marines on both ends of the bridge, now that they were there, and gradually built their strength until it was obvious that they were in complete control and were not going to move until things settled down between the two opposing Vietnamese forces. Along with the bridge we encompassed the ammunition dump that was also wired for destruction. We reasoned with the Vietnamese engineers this way: if we leave, there will be a fight between you and the government troops; if we stay, there will be no fight. In order not to discredit them (in accordance with the niceties of bargaining in the Far East), we agreed that they should guard the ammunition with us. It took several days, but in the end both bridge and ammunition were secure, and we turned to other worries.

By now we were deep into May. For almost three months we had walked a thin line between crises. We had seen four different general officers commanding the Vietnamese Army in our area, and used everything from old friendships to displays of naked force to keep some kind of order and circumvent armed clashes between the opposing factions.

The Buddhist organization had grown consistently in strength and now was the focal point of anti-government activities, to which they continued to add anti-American sentiment wherever they could. Hué remained the stronghold of the Buddhists, and the university students their shock troops. Anti-American riots were instigated, with cries of "Down with the American colonists!" The United States Information Service Library in Hué—devoted largely to textbooks for use by the students—was sacked and burned. And the confrontations between government and dissident units of the Vietnamese armed services continued. As much as possible we tried to stay out of the conflict, to let the Vietnamese work their problems out themselves. Sometimes we could not.

By late May the government effort against the Struggle Movement forces in Danang had lost much of its impetus. Dissident groups still held several strongpoints in the city, including fortified temples, and were well equipped with machine guns and other automatic weapons. The people of the city were caught in the chaos, with innocent civilians being killed and wounded as fighting flared up and subsided unexpectedly in various sectors of the heavily populated area. A few of these were Americans—there were over a thousand American civilians in Danang—but we had been able to keep them isolated from the actual street fighting.

There was much pressure from Saigon to end the Struggle Movement in Danang, and the local Vietnamese commander bore the brunt of it. On May 21 I learned that he intended to use the Vietnamese Air Force against the remaining pockets of resistance in the city. My concern for the safety of Americans in the city immediately increased. With caution, influence, and restraint we had kept American casualties extremely light and largely a product of accidental incidents. Now, with fast aircraft bombing and strafing into the city itself, many would be in grave danger from powerful weapons—bombs, rockets, high-explosive cannon—much less easy to control or isolate than small-arms fire on the ground.

I talked with the commander of the Vietnamese Air Force squadron at the Danang airbase, who told me quite simply that his orders came from Saigon and that he had been directed to support the attack with his planes.

The Vietnamese corps commander at the time was so fearful of his life at the hands of his own men that he was operating from the safety of my own headquarters. I told him of my concern and that I could not tolerate air attacks on Danang. He was most sympathetic but admitted that he had no control over the forces involved. When I received the information that propeller-driven Vietnamese attack aircraft were taking off from the Danang airbase with full loads of bombs and rockets, I told my own Marine Aircraft Wing commander to have four jet fighters stand by, armed with air-to-air ordnance.

The crisis came quickly. Two Struggle Movement machine guns placed near a Marine installation began firing on government troops. Two of the Vietnamese planes came in firing rockets, and three of the rockets fell short, into the Marine compound, wounding eight men, two seriously. I thereupon launched two of our own jets, and told them to orbit over the Vietnamese aircraft and be prepared to shoot them down on my order. I then informed the Vietnamese Air Force commander that I would have his planes shot out of the air if they fired one rocket, dropped one bomb, or shot one single round into the city.

A few minutes later I received a telephone call from Washington, informing me that they had a complaint from the Republic of Vietnam that I was interfering in their internal affairs. When I explained the situation, they agreed with my actions and told me to use my best judgment.

By the time the call was completed and I had informed General Westmoreland in Saigon (who was supporting me solidly), the Vietnamese had launched four more of their aircraft —to orbit above our two jets. I again called the Vietnamese Air Force commander, who informed me that if my jets fired on his planes beneath them, his planes above would shoot them down. I launched two more jets and stacked them over the latest Vietnamese arrivals.

For two hours this four-layer aircraft sandwich circled Danang, and I sat in my office with a telephone in each hand, one to the Vietnamese Air Force, the other to my air controller, who was in voice communication with the jets overhead. At last the Vietnamese tired of the waiting game and returned to base. To show our persistence—and continued resolve—we kept a two-plane jet patrol in the air over Danang for several days, but no Vietnamese aircraft entered the area again.

Toward the end of May all of the disjointed pieces that had plagued us since early March began to fall into place. Premier Ky came up from Saigon once again, this time to meet with General Thi, whose relief had triggered the holocaust of strife. They met, significantly, at our Marine airbase at Chu Lai, uninfluenced by the presence of any of the factions that had contributed to three months of strife. These were two old friends, both men of honor and both patriots. We gave them the courtesy of privacy, and I cannot say what transpired between them. I know only that it resulted in decisions.

On the last day of May 1966 General Hoang Xuan Lam, a young Vietnamese division commander in the I Corps, was made its commanding general. He was one who had remained aloof from all that had transpired, doing his soldier's job, keeping his troops busy and out of the internal political struggle. A big man for a Vietnamese, with a charming personality, exceptional personal courage, and complete dedication to his country, he assumed command of the Corps with one proviso: he would have no political responsibilities; let the civilians run the government and he would run the war.

Immediately upon assuming command he launched almost all of his forces into the field, their backs to the internal political struggle and their faces to the larger issues of the Viet Cong and the threat of invasion from the north. When the Buddhist faction and students of Hué seized advantage from the departure of Army units and made a vicious attack on the American Consulate there, gutting it with Molotov cocktails, the general turned two battalions of infantry around, re-entered the city and clapped on a tight, no-nonsense control. These troops and available armored units deployed to discourage major civil disorders and suppress minor disturbances, while the authorities reorganized police and municipal services, re-established the disrupted food and fuel supplies and gradually restored the city to normal.

Not long afterward Thich Tri Quang, the organizer and apparent head of the Buddhist political movement, was politely escorted from Hué to Saigon, where he remained under a watchful government. Finally, around June 21, the political struggle was over. Our Marines, through patience and very careful and considered application of force and threat of force, had managed to keep the lid on the very explosive situation in I Corps.

Even with several years of perspective on these events it would do little good to sort out and identify the many political, military, religious, and personal factors that led to and inflamed the series of crises in 1966. This much is plain: the fledgling government of Vietnam showed remarkable resilience under extreme pressure. Whoever it was that wanted it toppled was disappointed.

Also plain in retrospect is the complete abortion of the attempts to insert anti-Americanism as an issue. A group of six hundred students burned the American Consulate in Hué, and there were other anti-American acts, but the people—and the Vietnamese military—ranged from apathetic to hostile toward any anti-American acts. When it was over, the bonds between ourselves and the Vietnamese were strengthened. We had been together in the crisis and together we faced the future more closely than we had before.

The political struggle resulted in some high figures passing into exile or obscurity, but there was no purge against the ones beneath these few. And the Viet Cong had shown how weak and ineffective they were. All of I Corps—and the nation itself —had solidified again. What opportunity existed for the Viet Cong during those three long months, when we felt we were making no more headway but reeling from crisis to crisis, had been beyond their reach and now had disappeared. They had failed to capture the Struggle Movement, the Buddhist revolt, the Army, or the people.

In April 1966 the Vietnamese government announced plans for the popular election of a constituent assembly, to draft a constitution and schedule supporting elections for a national representative government. The Vietnamese people were about to demonstrate their own solid character and give the lie to "National Liberation."

The Viet Cong and North Vietnam fought against these elections with every weapon at their disposal. They broadcast warnings by radio, threatening the people of South Vietnam that anyone participating in elections would have to suffer awful consequences. They bore out their threats with assassinations and attempted assassinations of candidates, and with attacks against the people who went to the polls. Yet candidates stepped forward from among the people, and the people voted.

Through the national elections, down to the elections of village and hamlet officials, the terrorism continued—and the people continued to vote. They were wounded at the polling places and came back to vote with the bandages fresh on their wounds. They saw their candidates killed by Viet Cong, and voted for their replacements. Eighty-six per cent of those eligible voters who had registered cast their ballots in hamlet and village and town. (Compare that with the voting in your own community.)

Foreign cynics—including Americans—said they were forced to vote, but who could force a man to vote at the risk of his life? Foreign cynics—including Americans—said the elections would be rigged by a corrupt government, but who rigs an election for less than 39.1 per cent of the popular vote, which was the government party's total? All the sophistry faded before obscure little people who had to learn how to vote before they could cast their ballots, and did so, honestly and with resolve. All the terrorism and propaganda proved futile against a people too vastly concerned and too determined to express themselves to be deterred by threat of harm or harm itself.

The outlook for the Viet Cong was bleaker than ever. They

had lost militarily, they had lost politically. There was little more they could do within the country except to see their remaining strength ground down by increasingly powerful and increasingly confident forces, representing an increasingly stable and popular government. It was time for a reappraisal, not only in South Vietnam, but also in Hanoi; and the decision, whatever it was, would not be an easy one to make.

12

Ho Chi Minh's Regulars

The day before Christmas of 1965 we ceased fire for the second of what was to be a series of truces perforated by enemy violations. The bombing of North Vietnam was suspended for a month without noticeable reaction from Hanoi except for intensive repair efforts on their roads and bridges leading south. The Viet Cong and North Vietnam remained as intransigent as ever, demanding recognition of the National Liberation Front as a condition for slackening their own attacks.

There was little question, among those of us in the field at the time, that North Vietnam was fully in the war as a belligerent. The presence of her troops in the Republic of Vietnam was one of the precursors to our own entry. The distinctive helmets of North Vietnamese soldiers had been encountered within the Republic as early as 1964; there was good evidence that there were as many as nine regiments of regular North Vietnamese troops in South Vietnam by the beginning of 1966.

Yet our own northern sector—the area between Hué and the Demilitarized Zone along the Ben Hai River—was among the quietest in the whole Marine area. The 1st Division of the Army of the Republic of Vietnam, one of their best units, was in and around Hué and had kept the Viet Cong well off balance in both of the northern provinces of the Republic since our arrival.

American force was not entirely absent up by the DMZ, of course. Teams of Marines commonly accompanied the Vietnamese units to help them use the air and naval gunfire support available to them from our common resources. Marine reconnaissance teams, units of five to fifteen men, worked over the pleasant, rolling countryside, the dunes and paddies of the coastal flats, and the sharper slopes and heavier vegetation of the inland areas, as a screen of eyes and ears that kept us informed of events up north. The same screen of men was spread south a hundred miles or more, west of Danang and Tam Ky and Quang Ngai, like sensitive fingertips reaching out into fog. It was a waiting game.

Early in 1966 we began increasingly to encounter regular soldiers of the North Vietnamese Army, coming out of the western mountains with warm sweaters in their packs for use on the mountain trails that led from their own country to Laos and South Vietnam. They were sturdy, well-fed men with good weapons and equipment, uniformed, disciplined, and organized into companies, battalions, and regiments—a contrast in these respects to the guerrillas. Their entry marked a new phase of the war.

According to the rigid doctrine of the Communist Party, the attack on a nation begins with subversion, breaks into guerrilla warfare, and culminates in full-scale organized warfare—an Armageddon in which the enemy is annihilated. The subversion of the government of the Republic of Vietnam had developed into widespread guerrilla attack, but there the doctrine soured and grew rank. The magic formula was not working. The guerrilla was losing and a hard decision had to be made in Hanoi: retreat again into subversion or make a premature move into full-scale organized warfare.

Ho Chi Minh's Regulars

The decision—to invade the Republic of Vietnam with major forces from North Vietnam—was followed by months of preparation. Men and supplies had to be moved, mostly by foot, over hundreds of miles of primitive mountain and jungle trails. Food and ammunition had to be pre-positioned in selected battle areas. Bunkers and trench lines had to be dug; tunnels and caves excavated; roads and trails built; all by hand and mostly under the cover of darkness, rain, or fog. Finally they were ready.

On July 5, 1966, a Marine patrol captured a young Vietnamese soldier well north of Hué. He was healthy, confident, almost boastful. Ile said he was a member of a crack unit—the 324th "B" Division of the North Vietnamese Army—and only one of more than five thousand troops already in South Vietnam, with many more to come. General Giap and Ho Chi Minh had decided to slug it out with us.

There is an old Vietnamese maxim: *Biot minh biet nguoi, Tram tran danh tram tran thang*—"Knowing yourself and the enemy, you will win a hundred battles." It seemed this ancient wisdom had been buried beneath the thoughts of President Ho in Hanoi, for they did *not* know us very well. They had a good plan. They could, at best, seize the northern two provinces of the Republic of Vietnam, including the ancient capital city of Hué, and give much credence to a separate communist state within the country, further dividing Vietnam for enormous political as well as military gain.

They could—and did—force us to commit large numbers of our men to the north, weakening security and giving some relief to the hard-pressed guerrilla forces in other areas. They could—and did—vastly increase the bloodletting, accepting the heavy price upon their own people to impose casualties upon us and add to the war-weariness of the American people by skilled propaganda techniques. There remained, always, a

chance to effect some kind of dramatic victory, another Dienbienphu, that could trigger a collapse of the American will to
continue to fight.

Hanoi never thinks small. Its invasion of the two northern
provinces was only a segment of an overall design. Simultaneously with crossing the Demilitarized Zone in division strength,
they threw two divisions against the U.S. Army at Pleiku in the
central highlands and another out of Cambodia toward Saigon.

When armies clash, division against division, it is conventional war. Although battles may be fought by battalions and
regiments, the commitment of divisions means the application
of total resources: light and heavy artillery, tanks, motor transport, vast supply trains, and all the other equipage that spells
the difference between light infantry battle and sustained
heavy combat. This was a turning point in the conflict. Until
early 1966 my men had been widely dispersed, exercising the
greatest amount of security over the greatest number of people,
concentrating only when we found Viet Cong Main Force units
trying to bolster the hapless and struggling guerrilla, or to protect our most vital installations against guerrilla attack. Now
we were in a situation similar to that in Korea in 1950—an
army coming down from the north to seize and hold ground.

Quickly the battle was joined. I was able to free seven Marine infantry battalions; the Army of the Republic of Vietnam
provided five: twelve battalions of seasoned fighting men, well
supported with artillery and aircraft. The U.S. Seventh Fleet
moved in cruisers and destroyers to add to our firepower. We
created our own supply bases as we moved the units by truck
and helicopter and transport aircraft.

The infantry battalions fanned out into the area north and
west of Hué, toward the "demilitarized" zone that was now
honeycombed with supplies and troop shelters for the Army of
North Vietnam. We met them northwest of the city of Quang
Tri, capital of the northernmost province of the Republic, and

Ho Chi Minh's Regulars

there we fought. We found them well equipped, well trained, and aggressive to the point of fanaticism. They attacked in mass formations and died by the hundreds. Their leaders had misjudged the fighting ability of U.S. Marines and ARVN soldiers together; our superiority in artillery and total command of the air. They had failed to consider our naval ships offshore, and had vastly underestimated our mobility by air and men.

Their men were good in 1966—far better than later, when the price of poor judgment was paid over and over again by those bearing the brunt of battle in the field. They fought bravely and they fought well, and very few of them surrendered. Their men and ours slashed at each other by platoon and company, battalion and regiment, in dune and paddy and hill. When it was over, the 324th "B" Division of the North Vietnamese Army was back across the Demilitarized Zone, minus almost two thousand of its men, young men, born in the north to die in the south trying to impose the will of Ho Chi Minh on a free people. But they had accomplished two of their objectives: they had slowed the pacification of the I Corps area by forcing me to commit men into the largely barren north, and they had made many headlines in the United States about escalation and American casualties.

With the inflexibility of any totalitarian state, no real lesson was learned by North Vietnam as a result of this battle. They were committed to a course of action and they continued to follow it in spite of their casualties and the demonstration of their errors of judgment. In August and September they tried again, less boldly, hooking inland, crossing the Demilitarized Zone in and around the Laotian border, working eastward toward the coast through Quang Tri and Thua Thien Provinces, where we met them again in clash after clash, keeping them away from the coastal cities and forcing them back into the hills.

Ho Chi Minh's Regulars

There were hundreds of square miles to cover. We established fire-support bases, and worked from them under the cover of their protecting artillery: Cam Lo, Dong Ha, Con Thien, Gio Linh, strange names far away from Centreville and Bloomfield and Richwood and all the other places back home. The North Vietnamese attacked these places—as they attacked Khe Sanh later—seeking the Dienbienphu that was becoming increasingly important to them. And they failed each time, as they failed at Khe Sanh, leaving more bodies behind as they withdrew. We caught them in the open, time and again, and slashed at them with helicopter-borne assaults, keeping them from massing and keeping them on the move. We went into the valleys that led back into the mountains and were natural avenues from Laos to the coast—A Shau, Ba Long—and found their supply dumps and left them in ruins.

Gradually, with a continuous series of defeats and no Dienbienphu, with severe shortages of food and medical supplies, depleted strength of the combat units and constant harassment, the morale of these once aggressive regulars from North Vietnam degenerated, so that they became perceptibly more listless in their movements and attacks. Even the guerrilla they were trying to help by their sacrifices fell back upon hard times. The Marines we had sent north were replaced in the south by U.S. Army troops, and pacification continued behind the churning battles up by the DMZ. For, as we fought, we continued to work among the people of Vietnam.

And as we both fought and worked, the character of the local guerrilla changed. The Viet Cong Main Force underwent a transformation into North Vietnamese paramilitary units, with little local knowledge and without the local accent in their speech—no longer of the people, but imposed upon them. The whole nature of the National Liberation Front was now revealed for what it was from the outset: a pawn of Hanoi—and the people knew it.

Ho Chi Minh's Regulars

The decision made in Hanoi some time in 1966 was followed with true Party firmness. It did not give them a communist capital in South Vietnam or a province under communist rule. It did not result in any lasting reduction of the pacification of the country. It failed to help the guerrilla in his increasingly futile role, and it produced no Dienbienphu. It did get the kind of headlines in the United States that helped erode a little more of the will of our people to continue this strange war. Perhaps this modest result was worth the hundred thousand men or more to the leaders in Hanoi. It is too early now to say.

13

Deeds of
Mercy

Any story of the war in Vietnam is incomplete unless it examines the element of mercy that has been its particular hallmark for American participants and their allies. Because war is the province of suffering, the acts of compassion stand out starkly —and in Vietnam they are many and significant.

The very nature of the conflict, fought among a good people who are its principal victims, demands restraint. For Americans, the avoidance of noncombatant casualties is more than a directive: it is a constant theme. As a matter of both policy and preference we accept greater risks for ourselves in order to reduce the dangers to civilians.

Along with this are the annual ministrations to hundreds of thousands of fugitives from the Viet Cong and from North Vietnam; the medical care given freely throughout Vietnam to people who have suffered without doctors or nurses for their entire lives; care of the thousands of orphans, innocent victims of the war; the touching gift of normality to children disfigured by harelip or crippled with clubfoot.

Then, among our own, there are the chaplains and medical corpsmen, the doctors, and the helicopter pilots who pull the wounded men out of blazing battles and deposit them in minutes to the safety and care of a field hospital. This adds up to a miracle of medical care: Of a hundred wounded Marines, an average of thirty is treated in the field and returned to duty; thirty-five are treated in a hospital and returned to duty; five are evacuated to Okinawa or the Philippines and return to duty; thirty go back to the United States for extended treatment and care. Less than 2 per cent of the Marines wounded in Vietnam have died of their wounds.

Men who would have died of similar wounds as recently as the Korean conflict are now saved, not only by superior medical care, but also by the blessing of the helicopters and their superb pilots. The combat troops are not given to superlatives, but they unabashedly call the helicopters and the men who fly them "Angels of Mercy." There is hardly a place they have not gone or risks they have not taken to get the wounded out of battle and back to emergency care.

Capt. Richard Parks Louis Bland of Costa Mesa, California, was one such pilot. A reconnaissance team, deep in enemy territory west of Hué, had sustained a casualty and was in danger of being overrun by North Vietnamese troops they had been tracking. Flying a big transport helicopter, Captain Bland took off in bad weather that worsened as he went inland. When he reached the area of the patrol with the wounded man, the enemy had closed to within thirty yards of them, in dense jungle, and there were by this time several wounded Marines below.

As Bland directed the two armed helicopters that supported him into strafing and rocket runs on the enemy positions, he hovered his big plane over the jungle canopy and began to hoist the wounded men aboard, lowering a cable through the trees and reeling it into the waiting hands of his crew, all the while hovering above the treetops, enemy bullets flicking through his big ship. For forty minutes he held this precarious teeter-totter until all the wounded were aboard; then, nose down, he steered his battered helicopter through fog and rain to the nearest medical facility. Not done, he boarded another helicopter and returned to the hills to pick up the unwounded men, and was out on another mission before the day was over.

And there was Maj. Charles Henry Pitman of Chicago, plucking men off the edge of a forty-foot cliff in the dead of night, intermittent battle flares the only light, the rear wheels of his helicopter touching the ground, the front wheels hanging over the cliff, borne up only by the whirling rotor blades. In this dangerous perch, hovering against the side of a mountain in the dark, he jettisoned raw fuel down the abyss to lighten his ship so he could take all the waiting Marines aboard; then, heavily burdened, unable to lift off, he tipped the nose of his craft into the blackness below, down the steep mountainside, with enemy bullets snapping by, to gain forward speed and enough lift to soar out of the canyon and home again.

Determination, courage, skill, and selfless devotion to duty have always been the mark of the Naval aviator—which all Marine pilots are—but Vietnam is the first place where these qualities are displayed hundreds of times a week before the men on the ground. The bond between them and their flying opposites, always strong, has become stronger still, particularly through those sorties of mercy when the fragile helicopter is the lifeline to the wounded men or the last thin bridge to safety for an outnumbered and beleaguered unit.

It is not only to our own men and to Vietnamese combat troops that these aviators and machines are angels of mercy. The Vietnamese people know them too, and many of them owe their own lives to them: the refugees evacuated from combat areas and the depredations of the Viet Cong; the critically ill brought out of remote villages to expert medical care; the victims of natural disaster aided by the rushing blades of the helicopter when no other hope remains.

I remember the incident of a drowning fisherman, clinging to the mast of his sinking boat, the waves crashing over him, churned by thirty-mile-an-hour winds. Capt. Robert C. Marshall of Brooknead, Virginia, took off from Chu Lai in his helicopter, hovered over the lone figure desperately clutching the mast, and lowered a sling. Dragging the line through the water, Marshall maneuvered his plane until the sling was within reach of the fisherman. He grabbed it, but was too paralyzed by fear to let go of the mast. The helicopter pitched in the buffeting winds, fourteen-foot waves rushing below, battering at the Vietnamese.

Lance Cpl. Robert M. Conner, one of Marshall's crewmen, called on the intercom and told Marshall he would try to get the frightened man safely aboard. The sling was raised and lowered again with Conner in it. Sputtering and gasping, he was hauled through the turbulent water to the fisherman. Conner put his arms around the Vietnamese, who was still wrapped around the mast, and Marshall put power to the helicopter and tension on the singing cable. Like two olives coming off a toothpick, the men's grip slid up the slick mast until they were free to be hoisted aboard. Captain Marshall winged in toward the shore, another errand of mercy completed.

And there was Capt. Stephen Wesley Pless of Atlanta, Georgia. He was on a routine flight one day when an emergency call came crackling over the radio: a U.S. Army helicopter was down in a remote section of beach and was under attack by Viet Cong.

Captain Pless was flying a "gunship," a small, light helicopter specially adapted in Vietnam to carry a battery of machine guns and rockets. He had been escorting a regular transport helicopter to pick up a wounded Korean soldier. The two pilots talked it over briefly—terse, matter-of-fact voices over the radio—and agreed that Pless should go to help while the bigger plane went on its own way in the relatively quiet sector, its rotors churning the warm air on an errand of mercy.

Deeds of Mercy

Pless waved off and sped toward the beach, the nose of his plane slightly down, the paddyfields slipping to the rear like a great sheet of green silk rushing by. Once over the beach they headed south, Pless and his copilot, Capt. Rupert E. Fairfield, of Lake Charles, Louisiana, and a crew of two, their helicopter speeding down the beach like an angry hornet, its machine-gun muzzles sticking forward like stingers, the rocket pods slung underneath like the egg sacs of some huge insect, humming and dangerous.

The scene when they arrived was horrible. Four Americans, helpless in the sand, and thirty or forty Viet Cong about them, stabbing them with bayonets, beating them with rifle butts. Pless nosed his gunship almost to the ground and screamed by overhead, unable to fire but scattering the Viet Cong through sheer surprise. As they ran for the shelter of a treeline Pless whipped his little gunship back and opened fire, machine guns blazing and rockets flashing out of their tubes, hissing like side-winders. Over and over Pless pressed the attack, skimming in at treetop level and sometimes flying through the dust and debris of his own rocket explosions, and on one of those passes, he saw a weak arm wave, a gesture for help. At least one American soldier below was still alive.

The Viet Cong were firing back now from the shelter of the trees only yards away. Pless heard their bullets snap by as he landed, shielding the wounded man and the still forms of the other three soldiers with his helicopter, his crew chief piling out while Lance Cpl. John G. Phelps sprayed the dunes and trees with machine-gun bullets.

As the wounded man stumbled into the helicopter, Gunnery Sgt. Leroy N. Poulson checked the other bodies and found two of them still alive. He began dragging them through the soft sand to the helicopter. The copilot unstrapped himself and vaulted out of the helicopter to help. They fought off the Viet Cong with pistol and machine-gun fire as they piled the

[148]

wounded into the helicopter. Meanwhile, Captain Pless was still in the cockpit at the controls, waiting each second for that burst of fire that would take his life and turn his plane into a pyre. Three wounded men aboard. Captain Fairfield dashed to the remaining body—and shuddered: the Viet Cong had horribly mutilated him; he was dead.

Then help came. A U.S. Army gunship, a twin of Captain Pless's plane, arrived and took on the Viet Cong; a Vietnamese helicopter could be seen approaching over the water.

Captain Pless wasn't sure his little bird would fly with the wounded men aboard, but neither could they stay unless they wanted to end up like that grim body on the beach. Quickly they jettisoned their rocket pods and stripped the helicopter of any movable weight. Pless poured power to the laboring engine, and the overburdened helicopter staggered into the air. Heading for the open sea, away from the Viet Cong who were now on three sides of them, the helicopter slumped under the weight, and its landing skids splashed the water, then recovered. Nursing his heavily laden chopper, bouncing on and off the water like a stone skipped across a pond, his crew now giving first aid to the wounded men behind him, binding their bayonet wounds, Captain Pless forced his plane into enough forward speed so that they could rise above the waters and wing home—home with three soldiers wrenched literally from the jaws of death.

Such errands, gallant as they are, are only a segment of the total effort. Much of it is carried out by those elements of the United States Navy that are responsible for religious and medical support of the Marines: the Chaplain Corps and the Medical Corps. Both have been with us for almost two hundred years; they are with us today in Vietnam, indispensable as ever and as dedicated to their own deeds of mercy as we must be to battle.

Deeds of Mercy

It would be presumptuous for me to explain the role of the ministry in Vietnam. That has been done in large part by Chaplain John O'Connor* and I hope by others who can equally illuminate the role of the military chaplain in the vortex of war. What I have to say is addressed only to the type of man we, the soldiers, have come to expect from the men of God of all faiths who accompany us. It is one small part of the reason we hold them in such respect and seek them out for relief from our own travail.

Chaplain Vincent Robert Capodanno of Richmond County, New York, had his own formula for knowing and serving the men of the infantry battalion to which he was attached: go out with them into the field, company by company; live with them in all the danger and tedium and bone-wearying work; stand the lone night watches with them, and be with them in the heat of battle when it came.

It was September, a hot month in Vietnam, and it was M Company's turn to be up in the lead. Chaplain Capodanno went with them on a clear, bright day, the temperature in the nineties, humidity in the eighties, and a slight breeze coming over the gentle hills, rice fields, hedgerows, and brush. This had been Viet Cong country before they were chased back into the hills. Now the North Vietnamese had come down from the western mountains, three regiments of them or more, to make a show of force and harass the peasants and try to breathe some life into the moribund National Liberation Front. Two Marine batallions went to meet them—M Company included—and Chaplain Capodanno along to live for a while with one fifth of his "parish."

The meeting of the two forces was something like two blind scorpions in a bottle, only over an area five miles in diameter and involving five thousand men. Until it sorted out into some

* *A Chaplain Looks at Vietnam* (New York: World, 1968).

[150]

kind of pattern in which either commander could make a rational decision, it was a platoon and company war, sudden encounters in the broken, intermittently cultivated countryside, brush and scrub, valley and hill.

M Company made contact early, with one platoon engaged, and the chaplain moved forward toward the fight, calm and confident, attending the wounded with dignity and priestly demeanor, administering last rites to the dead as he found them on the battlefield—words of faith and dignity above the sound of battle. Soon the execution of his office as a chaplain brought him to the forefront of the fight, where he used his young strength to pull or carry wounded and dead men into the shelter of a fold of ground, into a little temporary chapel only feet away from the slashing bullets but sanctified for a moment at least by his presence and faith.

Mortar fire and grenades burst as the opposing forces closed, and singing fragments of hot metal tore off part of the chaplain's hand as he worked under the increasing fire, moving always to the hottest part of the fight, where the men of his scattered parish were dying on the hillslopes or writhing in pain from their wounds.

The battle was more cohesive now: more Marines were moving in on the enemy from their flank, gaining the upper hand—but the local fight raged on. Chaplain Capodanno saw an almost typical scene of Marine battle: a Navy medical corpsman rushing to a wounded Marine, the corpsman hit almost as he arrived; and a Marine moving up to cover the wounded corpsman, partly with his own body, partly with his rifle fire. Men of his own parish, wounded, dying, perhaps dead in the heat of the battle, in a little valiant knot on a scarred slope. Chaplain Capodanno, armed only with his faith, moved out, his bleeding hand unbandaged, and when the enemy machine-gun bullets cut him down, his torn hands were only inches from the wounded corpsman.

Deeds of Mercy

Lieutenant Capodanno was typical of the chaplains of all faiths. The officers and men of the Navy Medical Corps similarly know no bounds of dedication or devotion to duty. From the young man in his teens in the field with a Marine patrol, through the field hospitals, the gleaming hospital ships offshore, to the superb facilities and skills of the Naval hospitals in the United States, we are provided with the finest medical service in the world. The most real image of this superb service is where our own troops see it—young "Doc," with his first-aid kit and surprising bag of skills.

The episodes of their heroism are too numerous: men who disregard their own injuries to continue to treat the wounded Marines; a single corpsman crossing a fire-swept rice paddy eight times, each time bringing back a wounded Marine; a mortally wounded corpsman stretched on a slope of hot, dusty earth, the life bubbling out of his own body, continuing to treat the wounded until he died. There was a corpsman, attached to a Marine platoon in September 1966, who crawled from one wounded man to another, giving them first aid, with a piece of shell fragment in his own belly; and another a few days later who saved a Marine's life by emergency treatment while shielding his body from grenade blasts with his own back.

During lulls in the fighting, and in the quieter areas, the Navy Medical Corps is no less busy in Vietnam. They are one of the mainstays of our civic action effort, providing vital medical treatment and services to the Vietnamese, building a people as they build good will. The sick who have been made well, the suffering who have been relieved of pain, the crippled or deformed who have been made whole will never forget them, or the Americans, or their government, which made it possible through their cooperation and assistance.

Nor will the people of Vietnam forget that their children have been given an expanded life with our help. The medical care, the improvement in sanitation, the increased protein in the diet are building a nation, not just individual bodies.

There are more than five times as many children attending school in South Vietnam today than there were in all of Vietnam—north and south—at the time the Republic of Vietnam became an independent nation. These children are the future of Vietnam, for they will be its leaders. Each brick we place to build a school, each writing tablet we provide a child is a lasting contribution. This is why, in the midst of war, we have helped them add eighteen thousand new classrooms to their school systems during the last five years, and why the Viet Cong try to destroy them. This is why we are supporting dozens of orphanages, eliciting help from groups such as International Orphans, Inc., and using donations received by our chaplains to help give these children as much of a chance in the new Vietnam they will inherit as those who have parents. This is why the Marines have built and support children's hospitals at Dong Ha and Hoa Khanh, and keep a scholarship fund for young Vietnamese.

For Vietnam needs all of the talent and human energy it can develop during the years ahead. We will not always be there; they will. We have tried to bring them more than was needed just for war. It is to be hoped that when it is all over, the deeds of mercy in Vietnam will outlast the effects of the war itself.

Not too long ago a Marine patrol clashed with a strong force of North Vietnamese, and a medical corpsman was captured. He was bound and with two guards was marched back in toward the mountains. An airplane saw the three figures from above and, unaware that one was an American, let loose a barrage of rockets. The blast hurled the corpsman some distance and killed the two guards. Still bound, dizzy from the shock, he staggered down the mountain and collapsed into the stagnant water of a rice paddy, deep in hostile country. Dimly, he later recalled being dragged and carried, half-conscious, for an unknown period of time. He awoke in an American truck convoy. They had found him, carefully placed in sight along the road, obviously by a Vietnamese. The deeds of mercy are not all our own.

14

Watch on the Ben Hai

The Demilitarized Zone between North Vietnam and the Republic of Vietnam is six miles wide. It starts at the mouth of the Ben Hai River where it empties into the South China Sea and follows that watercourse west and inland until it dwindles into upland tributaries. From there it cuts back to the Laotian border in a straight line overland, in the fashion of boundaries made by men who draw lines on maps in the confines of air-conditioned offices, with a cavalier disregard for mountains or valleys, or toward lesser men who tread the ground instead of drawing neat lines on maps.

Nevertheless the zone is there, the product of an agreement reached at an international conference held in Geneva in 1954. The United States, as already noted, did not join in this agreement, although we formally assured the conference in Geneva that we would not interfere in its implementation. The State of Vietnam (predecessor to the present Republic of Vietnam) flatly refused to accept it because of unfair provisions for elections. Yet both of us respect the Demilitarized Zone far more than the Accords' signator, North Vietnam.

To the men who fight the battles along this line, the DMZ is a physical thing, not a cartographic abnormality or a legal conundrum. At the mouth of the Ben Hai it is a bleak expanse of sand and dune, scrub brush and palmetto, glaring hot and infested with insects. Farther inland the country is still flat but greener, the river broad and tepid, bordered by paddyland, small farm plots, and an occasional hamlet. West, this more pleasant country turns into savannah and rolling hills, increasingly steep and increasingly wooded with tropical vegetation; here you lose the river and encounter the beginnings of the true mountains, those limestone ridges weathered by a million years of rain, overgrown with vine and bush and tree, fissured and rotten, dotted with caves. This is the country across which the neat map line was drawn, from the headwaters of the Ben Hai to the Laotian border, a jumbled mass of rock and stream, tangled wood, and great canopies of overhanging branch.

Almost sixty miles, from ocean to mountain, from beach to jagged peak, the DMZ exists, with fifty thousand North Vietnamese regulars trying to break through to the population centers along the coast and half that number of Marines blocking their way. This is the watch on the Ben Hai, the screen of flesh and steel behind which a nation is cleansing itself of terror and building its hoped-for future in the community of free nations.

It is no easy task. The enemy moves from mountain fastnesses, some of them secreted in Laos, or from the privileged sanctuary of North Vietnam across the Ben Hai, choosing his own time and place of battle, massing his troops and supplies over many months, always seeking that one time he can trap and annihilate a major American force.

These are no guerrillas. They are regular soldiers, organized into battalions and regiments and divisions. They have Soviet and Chinese artillery that can hurl a six-inch shell eight miles, modern antitank guns, recoilless rifles, barrage rockets, mines, and demolitions. This enemy is the invader, pushing across the Ben Hai and meeting us in battle in South Vietnam. The principal battleground is northern Quang Tri Province, but the North Vietnamese have also traveled down the inland mountain chain to hit us from the west, and the Marines meet them in the hills and valleys west of Danang or Tam Ky; the U.S. Army meets them around Dak To and Pleiku; the Army of the Republic of Vietnam meets them at Loc Ninh and Tay Ninh—but our main frontier is the northern approach, the watch on the Ben Hai, and only the men who have done it know the skill and courage it takes.

The five-man patrol was about halfway between the coast and the Laotian border, four miles below the DMZ, looking for enemy troop movements. They had been out two days when they observed ten or fifteen North Vietnamese troops moving cautiously down from the mountains—too big a unit for a five-man patrol to handle, but small enough possibly to capture with a full Marine platoon. Softly the word was passed by radio, and not long afterward a column of helicopters came skimming over the rolling, partly open ground and debarked their troops in a broad semicircle—big, tough men in flak jackets and helmets.

All afternoon they searched through the stifling grass and brush without seeing an enemy soldier. Finally, with darkness approaching, the helicopters were called and began to lift out the tired infantry. This is always a dangerous moment and the Marines knew it. They pulled back into a circular defense, protecting a flat area where the helicopters could land, and began their withdrawal as fast as the choppers could flare in, with clouds of dust and flying debris, load troops, and take off again.

The enemy force they had been looking for was more than ten or fifteen men—it was ten times that—and it was well trained and well led. They too had endured the long, hot afternoon, holed up silently, and silently moving away from the Marines as they searched, belly down in the grass, the last man moving backward Indian-style, obliterating their trail. As the Marines fell back to their final perimeter the enemy moved in and waited while the helicopters came in and left, counting the loads as they departed, holding their fire with creditable discipline until only half the platoon remained on the ground and darkness was coming on fast. Then they opened fire.

The helicopters were the first to feel it, bursts of bullets ripping through their machines as they flared in for a landing. One twirled and collapsed sideways, rotor blades snapping off, crushing into the dusty grass; then another.

The remaining Marines on the ground opened up a furious fire, and the helicopters tried again, single bullets snapping by them and bursts of small-arms fire like the angry tearing of stiff paper. One settled heavily to the ground, crushing its own landing gear, the crew desperately pulling the bleeding pilot out of his cockpit. Another, riddled, slipped into the ground, spilling gasoline from its ruptured fuel cells. The cries of the North Vietnamese could be heard above the clatter and confusion of battle as they closed on the tightened little group of Marines, and the soft tropical night began.

Back at Dong Ha the company commander, Captain (now Major) Howard W. Lee, of New York City, listened with serious face to the messages coming in on the radio: the enemy is within grenade range of our position; he has rockets and machine guns; there are over a hundred, an estimated company of North Vietnamese regulars; we can hold until morning if we have more men; we need ammunition, ammunition, ammunition, and more men.

These were Captain Lee's men. He had sent them out. If anyone went to them, he would be along. He asked the Marine pilots: Can you try it again, just a handful of us, with ammunition? The pilots thought of the crushed and burning machines out there, the dead and wounded of their own squadron alongside those of the infantry in the dusty grass, and of the twenty-one Marines back to back in the night with a North Vietnamese company assaulting their position, and they said, Sure; we might make it with two of the little choppers, the Hueys, fast and light, more maneuverable, with less inflammable fuel than the aviation gas of the big birds; sure, we'll give it a try.

So Captain Lee and three men and all the ammunition they could load on the Hueys swirled into the little perimeter in the darkness of early evening. Eager hands grabbed for the ammunition, and Lee took over. Now it was E Company of the 4th Marines out there, the old 4th that used to be in China before Captain Lee was born, that had known Bataan and Corregidor, tougher nights than this one in Vietnam.

The North Vietnamese attacked again, hurling grenades, and the newly arrived ammunition blazed in the hands of determined men. Lee went down, severely wounded, but conscious and still in command. The enemy, unable to break the firm little ring of men, fell back, and Lee took the reports: so many men killed, so many men wounded, and ammunition low again. Now it was his turn on the radio—ammunition, ammunition, ammunition.

Just before midnight another Huey came streaking in out of the dark sky, its belly full of ammunition. The North Vietnamese were ready, and it wobbled and slumped under their fire, pancaking into the perimeter, a wounded bird flopping into the ground. The pilot and crew piled out, helped the anxious defenders unload the precious cargo and reported to Captain Lee: Looks like we've joined the infantry, Captain—got anything we can shoot? Quietly they took their positions, and E Company, now reinforced by three aviators from the Marine Air Wing, was back up to twenty men under a wounded captain.

When dawn came, they were still there, and among the enemy bodies strewn about their position was that of the North Vietnamese company commander.

Watch on the Ben Hai

When it dresses up, the 5th Marine Regiment wears a *fourragère* won in World War I. Although its men who guard the DMZ often have never seen the proud award, they act with the special spirit of an elite unit within an elite corps. Lance Cpl. Richard A. Pittman of Stockton, California, was one of these.

It happened back in the mountains, along a narrow jungle trail near the vaguely defined DMZ. The whole company was on the move, "I" Company (they called it "India" Company, as in the phonetic alphabet) of the 5th Marines, with the second platoon in the lead, Pittman's first platoon next. The crash of fire came suddenly, breaking the cautious stillness and echoing from the surrounding hills. Then the ringing shock of mortar fire joined the clatter of small arms.

Pittman's group, not under fire, but close behind the fight, deployed and took cover. As they waited the dead and wounded from the leading platoon were brought back up the trail, past Pittman and the rest of the waiting men. Dimly he heard the men ahead crying, "More firepower, more firepower!" Waiting no longer, Pittman dropped his rifle, grabbed a machine gun and several belts of ammunition, and moved up the trail to the heavily hit unit ahead.

Moments later he came under fire himself, and cut his way through the enemy with broad arcs of bullets, the glistening brass cartridges slipping into the receiver of his weapon from the belt looped over his shoulder and spitting out of the muzzle, tearing the trees and bush to either side of him. Moving through, still firing, he was attacked by two automatic weapons, and silenced them with long bursts of fire. On and on up the trail, past Marines firing to either side, up to the head of the platoon, where the first men had fallen.

There, among the dead and wounded, the enemy attacked him, thirty or forty of them, dashing boldly down the trail, stocky little men in khaki uniforms, armed with submachine guns. Pittman planted his feet in the middle of the trail and poured fire at them from the gun at his hip, fired until the heated gun jammed, grabbed a fallen Marine's submachine gun and emptied it at them, grabbed a pistol and emptied it also, then, panting, groping, found a grenade, pulled its pin, and hurled it at the fleeing enemy, those men from North Vietnam invading the south and fleeing from Lance Corporal Pittman, who had never heard of Belleau Wood or worn the *fourragère* of the 5th Marine Regiment.

The hill was fifteen hundred feet high and the Marine platoon on top of it was only eighteen men commanded by a platoon sergeant, Jimmie E. Howard, of Burlington, Iowa. It was one of the many vantage points from which a few men could spot enemy movements over a huge area and keep the North Vietnamese from massing for attacks down the valleys or ridges toward the coast. It is a dangerous game, for you can hide men but not a hill. Although the enemy may try several hills without finding a living soul on them, he can just as well hit the one you're on—and that is what happened to Sergeant Howard and his men on the night of June 16.

They were North Vietnamese and there was about a battalion of them. They had skirted the DMZ, coming down the inland mountain trails, and were trying to work out to the coastal region. And Sergeant Howard's men were in their way. It had taken the invaders most of the night to clamber up the slopes in the dark, and they assaulted in the early-morning hours, with mortar fire, machine guns, and quick-firing automatic rifles.

Howard and his men were almost overrun in the first assault. Quickly he pulled them together into a tight defensive perimeter. Lance Cpl. John T. Adams, of Portland, Oregon, didn't make it. He had poured rifle fire at the assaulting hordes of enemy soldiers until his weapon was empty and, with no time to reload, waded into their ranks, using his rifle as a club, beating down two more before he was struck down by automatic-weapons fire. Cpl. Jerrald R. Thompson, of Palmer, California, didn't make it either. On the way he was felled by a hand grenade. Mortally wounded, at bay, he met the oncoming enemy with a naked sheath knife, and killed two of them before he died, there in the night, on a numbered, nameless hill in South Vietnam.

Sergeant Howard and sixteen men closed together to fight it out with a battalion of North Vietnamese. Coolly, professionally, Howard called for artillery support, and soon the long, tearing rustle of incoming shells and their bursts among the enemy there in the darkness were comforting. He called for flares, and they came, lighting the hill and surrounding countryside with millions of candlepower. The Marine jet bombers came in to help, and the little helicopter gunships, pouring rockets and machine-gun fire, bombs, and cannon shell into the surrounding enemy force.

The North Vietnamese attacked the hilltop again and again, shooting and hurling grenades. Sergeant Howard was painfully wounded, unable to move his legs—he gave all his ammunition to his men and stayed on the radio, unarmed, calling in artillery fire and air strikes, still in command, keeping up his men's spirits, steady as the rocks to which they clung. Ammunition ran low, and Howard told his men to laugh at the North Vietnamese, to throw rocks as if they were grenades—crazy Americans on a hill, confusing the enemy, keeping them off balance until the dawn.

Finally, first light came. Sergeant Howard and twelve men were still alive, but only one was unwounded. The rescue helicopters were ready at dawn, but Howard told them to wait—wait for one last strike at his tormentors, and he brought it in with vengeance, the blood from his wounded legs sopping the bandages as he directed the aircraft in broad daylight now,

Watch on the Ben Hai

pouring fire at the fleeing battalion. Then the choppers came in and lifted out the men, the dead and the wounded, leaving behind the battered, barren hill and the remnants of a North Vietnamese battalion.

Such is the watch on the Ben Hai, by men of fortitude equal to any we have known in our history. They are supported by every means at our disposal: all the power of the Marine Aircraft Wing, as well as Navy and Air Force air support; both Marine and Army artillery; B-52 strikes; Navy-Marine amphibious forces offshore; destroyers and cruisers of the Navy offshore. In spite of all this power, there must be steadfast men on the ground itself to block the way. In former days the ramparts they watch would be known as the northern marches of a frontier; today they are guarding the frontier of all free men against despotism. Some of them die, and we mourn their death, but it were better that the well-meaning people who read their names on the steps of our Capitol read instead the principles for which they gave their lives.

15

Call of
Duty

On June 1, 1967, I turned over my command to my successor and the following day boarded a plane for the return trip to the United States. It had been two years and six days since my arrival in Vietnam.

I left with regret. If it had been my choice, I would have stayed for the same reason that so many others have stayed beyond their required tour of duty in Vietnam. I too had identified with the conflict there and believed in what we were doing. Instead, the call of duty took me to Washington, where I have been as deeply concerned with the continuing events in Southeast Asia as if I were still there. Twice each year I have returned to Vietnam for several weeks at a time, to see for myself what is transpiring and to clarify with my own observations what I meanwhile have learned in Washington.

I have also been able to review with some perspective what went on in Vietnam while I was involved with the daily problems of command, and privileged to discuss both the war itself and the broader issues with many people, military and nonmilitary. In my daily work I have had the assistance of loyal and competent men and women to help me review the masses of information that constantly come from and about Vietnam.

There have been many critical events during the past three years: the protracted battle around Khe Sanh; the enemy's bold offensive during the traditional Tet holiday in February of 1968; the allied offensive that followed that aborted attempt to seize political control of the Republic; the destruction of enemy base areas throughout 1969; the commencement of American troop withdrawals as the enemy weakened and the Republic of Vietnam strengthened; then, in 1970, the not unexpected reaction of a frustrated North Vietnam turning on her other neighbors in Southeast Asia, Laos and Cambodia, trying to accomplish by further aggression what she had failed to do in South Vietnam. Meanwhile, all through these major events, the inexorable decision was being made throughout Vietnam, not by generals, but by an election in a village, a foot patrol, an ambush, or a small shop started by a peasant's son, and by a Viet Cong bringing in his weapon to fight no more unless it be for—not against—the government of the people of the Republic of Vietnam.

These last events are the reality, often more so than what we read in the daily paper or see dramatized for us on television. If each of us could see through the air of despair, the pressures for surrender that encompass us, we would recognize more clearly that the area under absolute control of the Viet Cong had shrunk to about 7 per cent of the country by 1970. The guerrilla bands I knew in 1965—that shadow government that ruled the counrtyside from sunset to sunrise—have withered in numbers, strength, and above all in their ability to intimidate the people.

In late 1969 Sir Robert Thompson, a British military authority on guerrilla operations in the Far East, made a five-week tour of investigation in South Vietnam for President Nixon. He saw, as I have seen, the erosion of Viet Cong influence in the countryside. He wrote:

Call of Duty

I was able to visit areas and walk through villages which had been under Viet Cong control for years. There was a much greater feeling of security, and the people were ready to take up arms for the government because they sensed that the Viet Cong were weaker. . . . Village people no longer build foxholes for their own protection in case of a firefight. On roads which had been completely deserted except for military convoys in the period after the Tet offensive, there is now a constant stream of civilian traffic. Existing roads are kept open, and more are being repaired and opened monthly.*

Such observations are strangely different from the general impression of the Vietnam war obtained by the citizen at home. This difference in outlook was so marked, when I first encountered it on my return to the United States, that it became my principal compulsion to write what I had seen and known. My access to the facts about the war in Vietnam has been constant and ample since 1965. I have been back to that country five times since that day in June I flew home. I have seen and read the bad as well as the good. I have experienced disappointments and chagrin, surprise and shock, sorrow and regret, but my optimism about the ultimate outcome has grown over the years.

Today, in 1970, the ability of the communist north to take over the republic to the south is minimal. The Viet Cong have lost not only almost all their former power; they have lost as well the mystique of the guerrilla and the myth of revolution. If anyone doubts who is fighting the free nations in Southeast Asia today, let him go to Vietnam or Laos or Cambodia and see the regular soldiers of North Vietnam in action. These are not

* Sir Robert Thompson, "On the Road to a Just Peace," *Reader's Digest,* March 1970.

guerrillas, nor is what they are doing revolution. This is a regular army, and it is *invasion*.

Even in the face of this, the Republic of Vietnam is stronger than we ever imagined it would be in 1965. What is more, the government that has been so vilified over the past few years that most Americans regard it with suspicion is increasingly proving itself to its own citizens and increasingly drawing their trust. The national economy is expanding and the evidence of it is plain to the little man as well as to the big one. The people of the Republic can regard with growing confidence a country of their own, a government of their own, and a future over which they, as a people, will have a decisive measure of control. But large segments of American public opinion seem unaware of or indifferent to this progress. Certainly they have drawn the wrong conclusions from many key events.

I can remember, for instance, talking to thousands of our countrymen while the Marines in Vietnam were deeply involved in the fighting around Khe Sanh. Most of them at home thought of it as a siege of an American garrison, potentially another Dienbienphu. It was nothing of the sort.

I have been in and out of Khe Sanh many times. I placed the first American troops—some of my own Marines—there, knowing that we could walk in and out if we wished, or walk in with more men if we wished, whether the North Vietnamese Army liked it or not. A large number of Americans, both Marines and U.S. Army men, did just that in the spring of 1968, going from the coastal region all the way to the Laotian border and back again, along Route 9, through Khe Sanh each time.

The fighting around Khe Sanh has been variously depicted, and there remains a general public impression that we narrowly escaped a military disaster there. It was an easy impression to obtain. I was in Washington at the time and watched, with the average citizen, the dramatic pictures of our downed transport planes, their twisted fuselages pulled off to the side of the runway, while others landed or took off in a rain of enemy mortar or artillery fire. It seemed, at that distance, that we had an isolated garrison on our hands, trapped in the hinterland, surviving only by the tenuous and dwindling airlift, a slender thread about to snap.

This outlook, from the vantage point back home, became most bleak in March of 1968, at a time when, in fact, no one with full cognizance of the circumstances had any serious concern about the enemy overrunning Khe Sanh. That same month, as one crushed American aircraft loomed large in the eyes and minds of the American people, nine hundred aircraft went in and out of Khe Sanh; of these, forty-four were shot at, eight were hit, and only two were destroyed. There is no doubt that the enemy made every attempt to isolate and destroy our forces at Khe Sanh; but neither is there any doubt that it was a military disaster to him.

I do not know whether the attack on Khe Sanh was intended to occur simultaneously with the Tet offensive of February, or whether it was to be the *coup de grâce* of the war, as Dienbienphu was to the French in 1954—a devastating blow to our home morale that would bring us to the conference table abjectly suing for peace. I do know this: the enemy lost twelve thousand men at Khe Sanh, the defenders lost two hundred; the defense of Khe Sanh kept two North Vietnamese divisions—twenty thousand men—from Hué, while their own beleaguered garrison in the Citadel of that city was isolated and destroyed; and the enemy found himself exposed at Khe Sanh to such overwhelming artillery and air power, deliverable under all conditions of night and day and weather, that his own strategy became a calamity. I know also what too many Americans at home were not told clearly enough to register, that South Vietnamese forces were at our side in large numbers at Khe Sanh.

What concerned me most during the fight around Khe Sanh

was not related to any feelings of a beleaguered fortress reminiscent of *Beau Geste*. It was, rather, something unnoticed by most of our public at the time. Fifteen miles to the east of Khe Sanh a full division of regular North Vietnamese troops crossed the Demilitarized Zone not too far from the coast. We met them there—Marines and the U. S. Army and ARVN—and we defeated them around Quang Tri City and Hué. We rolled them back with over five thousand fewer men than they had started with—half their strength. A battle almost unnoticed in the furor over Khe Sanh, although much bigger and vastly more important. This typifies the curiously distorted prism through which we daily view the struggle.

Another and even more striking example of the wide disparity of view between the people and those whom they hold responsible for the conduct of the war and the lives of their sons was provided by the enemy's Tet offensive in early 1968. The average American, especially when the impact of the event was still fresh on our nerves, saw that offensive as a stunning blow to our side. Yet I have always considered it—as do virtually all informed analysts—a great disaster to the enemy, not to ourselves or the Republic of Vietnam.

We know that he lost more than twenty thousand men in I Corps alone during February and March, with sixty-four thousand killed and ten thousand captured throughout the country. We know also that these men were vital to him; not only the North Vietnamese regulars but also the village guerrilla and hamlet activist, the communist underground, the Viet Cong administrators, tax collectors, recruiters, guides and scouts and intelligence agents. All of them had been staked for the great offensive.

The regulars were Hanoi's blue-chip troops, sent to capture cities without a plan for withdrawal. You do not replace such men in months or even years. You do not expend them against regular troops in frontal attacks unless you are desperate. So I thought then, and think now, that the Tet drive was an act of desperation. It was brilliantly planned and executed, but proved a colossal failure—except in one respect: its psychological impact on the people of the United States.

The government of the Republic of Vietnam did not fall as a result of the Tet offensive; the people were not panicked into submitting to communism. On the contrary, the offensive was the "Pearl Harbor" of South Vietnam: it solidified and strengthened the people and brought them closer to their own government and armed forces than they had ever been before.

The morale of the armed forces of the Republic soared as a result of their trial and their astonishing victories during the Tet offensive. They had reason to be proud of their defense—and subsequent counterattacks. It is too easily forgotten that Hué was recaptured by Vietnamese as well as by Americans, that there were thirteen battalions of the Army of the Republic in that fight alone, and they lost almost four hundred men in their attacks. It is also often forgotten that the South Vietnamese armed forces cleared the enemy from thirty-four of the thirty-six major cities with little or no help from their allies. It was without doubt the turning point in the military conflict, and entirely in South Vietnam's favor.

At the same time there is no question that the Tet offensive, coming after three years of American involvement and years of grinding, patient effort at pacification, was a master stroke of propaganda, despite its debacle in military terms. Sir Robert Thompson, in the article already quoted, reaches the same judgment: While "a disaster for them in South Vietnam," he writes, "the Tet offensive was a traumatic psychological victory for Hanoi and the Viet Cong in the realm of American public opinion." Who can forget the waves of pessimism that swept the United States after the initial weeks of disastrous reports? Indeed, I doubt whether we as a people have ever quite recovered from it. Certainly, in terms of morale, we have made less of a recovery than the people of South Vietnam.

Neither has the enemy recovered from his own offensive. There is one peculiarity about communist leadership that I have noted in both the Korean and the Vietnamese war: their planning may be excellent, but its execution is hampered by almost total inflexibility. The communists seem incapable of recognizing that even the best plan can go awry, and consequently are unprepared to deal with failure. Perfection is assumed, expected, and demanded by the supposedly omniscient Party. As a result, any failure is bound to be repeated again and again in diminishing strength, doomed each time to further failure. The Party cannot acknowledge or make contingency plans for error.

That is how it was in Vietnam, after Tet. The decimated ranks of the faithful tried it once more in May of 1968, now against alerted allied units, and failed again.

The decision had been made by Hanoi in 1966 to meet our powerful new forces in conventional combat, regiment against regiment, division against division. Then, in late 1967, General Giap, reading his own book, had decided on moving into the final phase of guerrilla warfare: his Phase III—full-scale organized warfare. It was launched in early 1968. Obviously, he had dreams of a new Dienbienphu—at Khe Sanh or Pleiku or Con Thien. The dreams foundered on the shoals of American and allied resistance and counterattack. Now, four years of bloodletting gone by, the brunt of the battle was passed back to the guerrillas—except that many of them were no longer there, victims of their own fatigue and disenchantment, victims of the leaders who threw them into the open against machine guns during Tet.

The Communist Party cannot be wrong, so the regular North Vietnamese soldiers were used to flesh out the thin ranks of the remaining guerrilla bands—fourteen- and fifteen-year-old boys from the north, with a different accent from the southern peasant's, who knew the countryside no better and often less well than our own men. Today, in I Corps, the guerrilla units are nearly three-quarters filled with North Vietnamese regulars; some of them are almost entirely North Vietnamese.

The regular battalions we are encountering in the bush are severely weakened by this additional burden, so many of their men being scattered in guerrilla units. Many replacements from the north are going into guerrilla bands instead of into the regular units. Combined, regular and guerrilla, these forces are less effective than the guerrilla and Main Force Viet Cong were in 1965 or 1966. While we can do infinitely more now than we could four years ago, theirs is the dismal knowledge that four years of sacrifice have left them too weak to do more than harass the powerful forces that thwart them and punish the civilian population that has turned its back to them.

What, I have been asked, of the Viet Cong rocket that tears through the air almost any night and crashes into Saigon or Danang or an American base in South Vietnam? This is intended to announce that the enemy can strike at will, any time, any place, and all our vaunted efforts against him are futile.

When I was very young, there was a German gun called Big Bertha that could shoot seventy-five miles—just enough to lob shells into Paris at extreme range. From the Battle of the Marne in 1914 to the Ludendorff Offensive in 1918, German armies had threatened Paris and Allied armies had defended it. Big Bertha was expensive, inaccurate, and ineffective—a weapon of spite, inflicting random damage to relieve the frustration of being able to do no better.

When I was much older, there were the German V-1 and V-2 rockets. One was a pilotless airplane that headed in the general direction of England and crashed with its bomb load; the other was the first ballistic missile rocket, tipping up into the iono-sphere and plunging toward London. These, too, were spite weapons, no matter how technically ingenious. They were used, as Big Bertha had been used, to relieve somewhat the frustration of being able to do no better.

When I was considerably older, I was concerned about the security of the huge airbase at Danang. The biggest weapon we knew that the Viet Cong had in 1965 was the 81-millimeter mortar with a range of over two miles. Painstakingly we extended a ring of tight security beyond that distance. One night, much later, mortar rounds came crashing down on the base, rather idiotically on the bare center of the concrete runway, with a few thrown in the general direction of a Seabee camp and hospital. The next morning one of my officers brought a mangled tailfin to me—a Chinese-made 120-millimeter mortar shell, with a range of over three miles. Painstakingly again we extended our area of tight security more than three miles from the airbase.

The Army was encountering the same thing at Pleiku and Qui Nhon and other places. The armed forces of the Republic were experiencing it at Saigon and Quang Tri and Hué. There, too, defensive adjustments were quickly made to deal with the longer ranges.

As the enemy was pushed farther and farther into the hinter-land, even his longest-ranged mortars became useless to him. He was unable to use artillery except from the privileged sanc-tuary of North Vietnam, for we could—and did—destroy or capture those brought into the Republic of Vietnam. As the Germans did with England in 1944, the enemy in Vietnam went to rockets—simple, direct-fire rockets with shockingly poor accuracy but respectable range: first, 140-millimeter rock-ets with a six-mile range; then, as even these became inade-quate, to 122-millimeter rockets with a seven-mile range.

Like Big Bertha and the V-2, the Chinese- and Russian-made

rockets plunge into Vietnamese cities with a sound like the tearing of a windowshade, exploding randomly into hut and street and square. These are spite weapons, weapons of frustration, admissions of weakness. They cause casualties—overwhelmingly noncombatants—and make dramatic stories for your morning paper, but the greatest value they have for the enemy is in their uplift to the sagging spirits of his men, and as a morale weapon directed at the world generally and our own people especially.

For over a year now our military operations in Vietnam have been a combination of local security for the people and a stamping-out of enemy base areas in the mountains and jungle inland.

The war against the guerrilla has been unending, but the results are seen with more clarity each passing year. In 1965 eleven thousand Viet Cong soldiers and supporters surrendered voluntarily to the government or to allied forces. In 1966 twenty thousand surrendered. In 1967 twenty-seven thousand surrendered. In 1968 eighteen thousand surrendered and more than ten thousand were captured. This was the year of the Tet offensive—the year when General Giap brought the guerrilla fighter into the open in what was to be the decisive battle; the battle, as it turned out, in which sixty-four thousand young Vietnamese were sacrificed to the Party in a two-month period. *But during 1969 more than forty-seven thousand formerly hostile people surrendered to the Government of the Republic of Vietnam.*

Such is the state of the enemy's forces. These are not men killed or wounded or captured. These are people disenchanted with a system they have fought for and know, people who are making a free choice between systems. Hundreds of them bring their weapons with them, weapons with which they have killed Americans and Vietnamese, weapons they refuse to use any longer.

[174]

Call of Duty

Our own operations in the last two years have cut deeply into the material assets of the Viet Cong and North Vietnamese Army forces in the I Corps area of South Vietnam. There is no hill so high or valley so deep that we cannot enter it at will, from the East China Sea to Laos. During these two years our combined forces found more than fifty-seven thousand weapons in arms caches or littering the battle areas where enemy forces had been found and fought. Today, in 1970, the allied forces continue their pressure on base areas of the enemy, once tucked back into the inviolate mountains and valleys, now falling one by one into our hands.

The A Shau Valley has long been a way-stop for men and supplies coming down through Laos and entering Vietnam from the west. It is a rugged place, over a thousand feet above sea level, with mountains looming even higher to east and west. Battalions of Marines, U.S. Army, and ARVN troops have been in and through its vastness since January of 1969. They have found thousands of weapons—rifles, submachine guns, machine guns, hundreds of the rockets that fall spitefully into Vietnamese cities, new trucks, glistening new artillery pieces, and vast quantities of ammunition.

The enemy has fought for his matériel, brought down from China at enormous labor. "Hamburger Hill" is a rise some twelve hundred feet above the valley floor, and they held it to deny us our searches. But the men of the United States Army and those of the Army of the Republic of Vietnam took it from them, and denied them access to this strategic valley from which they planned to launch another attack on Hué. As a single battle for a hill far away from home, it sounded as senseless and brutal as all war; as a price in blood for materials of war that could kill a thousand—or ten thousand—men, women, and children at a later time or place, it has urgent and logical meaning. This is a reality that must be faced by men whose duty it is to face realities.

Call of Duty

On my visit to Vietnam in the late autumn of 1969 I found the same confidence that has always been present among our officers and men—a confidence in strange contrast with the bafflement and indecision so common at home.

The Army of the Republic of Vietnam was equally confident; they were on the move, and immensely proud of it, coursing through the remote valleys many miles inland, scouring the jungled hills, meeting the enemy on his own ground and defeating him in open battle with American fire power and mobility on their side. They had taken over the majority of the area once held by the 3d Marine Division, and our own men were starting back home.

I saw the local troops of the Republic—the Regional Forces and Popular Forces who used to do guard duty and defend old garrisons—now armed with our superb M-16 rifles, out in the jungle and paddy, moving against our common enemies and successfully engaging and defeating them. They impressed me as similarly confident, offensive-minded with a clear purpose to defend their own people at the hamlet, village, and district level against Viet Cong coercion or North Vietnamese invasion.

And a new element had entered the conflict: the people's Self-Defense Force. After the shock and struggle of the Tet offensive, the people went to their own government and asked for means to defend themselves and their families against such horrors.

There is a young couple in Hué, around twenty-five years old. I talked with them in May of 1968. They had two children —once there were three. During the Tet offensive a unit of the regular army of North Vietnam seized the part of the city where the young couple and their children lived. They were made prisoner by these troops from the north.

During the fight that developed our Marine Corps forces were called in and became heavily involved with the North Vietnamese Army, along the Perfume River, where the young

Vietnamese family was held. From where they were they could easily see the stream of helicopters going in and out and the wounded Marines being loaded aboard.

There was a tough young North Vietnamese captain who seemed to command their area, and this is what he did. He ordered them, first father and then mother, to shoot a rifle at the helicopters shuttling back and forth along the Perfume River. They refused. He told them to obey his order or he would kill their children. They still refused.

This captain of the regular army of North Vietnam, whose troops had invaded the ancient capital of Hué from across the Ben Hai River to the north, whose leader was Ho Chi Minh, and whose religion was Asian communism, then took the middle child—a five-year-old girl—and cut her throat before the eyes of her parents and her brother and sister. Horror piled on horror as the other two children—a boy of seven, a girl of three —were bound together with barbed wire and, screaming, hurled into a ditch. Last, the mother and father were trussed together, the barbed wire biting into their flesh, and in this awful last embrace they, too, were thrown into the ditch. When the Marines—sweaty, dirty, tired men, some with bandaged wounds—closed on the area in the chaotic embroilment of infantry battle, the young family was being *buried alive*.

This family, less the slain child, lives in Hué today. I heard of their rescue from my own Marines and I sought them out to hear it from their own lips. They were but one family out of many; five people out of thousands; for we are still uncovering mass graves filled with remains of Vietnamese civilians murdered in equally terrible ways during the communist occupation of Hué. Estimates of the number of victims—murdered in the course of one brief occupation of one city, on the basis of advance lists of "enemies" marked for "liquidation"—run to about a tenth of the Hué population! The same or similar things happened in Cholon and Saigon. The same could happen countrywide to millions, if the Republic of Vietnam collapsed under Communist attack.

These people, the little people of Vietnam, are now armed. They are the People's Self-Defense Force. The men and women of this organization are trained, organized, armed, and equipped by their government, at their own request, to defend their own hamlets, villages, and towns. This force now counts over 3 million members.

Each of these has committed himself irrevocably to his government and its principles, and done so in the face of an almost certain death—possibly by torture—if the Viet Cong or North Vietnamese ever obtain power over them. This is a grave decision for each individual; a decision few Americans will ever have to make. To realize that over 3 million people have made such a decision is to understand much about the progress of the war.

They may not look like much as soldiers, this People's Self-Defense Force. It would be easy for the uninformed to regard them with contempt or amusement. But whenever I see one, I think of the young father still alive who can remember bright blood gushing from the throat of his child, the press of his wife's body bound to him in their common grave, and the clods of earth as they showered down to close out the lovely sky— and I would dread to bear the banner of communism in his sight.

For the Vietnamese who bear arms as our allies are not to be taken lightly. They have suffered infinitely more and persevered for many more years than we. Since 1961 the armed forces of the Republic of Vietnam have lost more than one hundred and six thousand men killed in battle; their casualties in I Corps exceeded those of the U.S. Marines in 1969, and are exceeding them again in 1970. But this blood has not been spilled in vain.

On my most recent visit to the I Corps area I found the same unspectacular but steady improvement in the countryside that has always marked our operations there. Among 93 per cent of the people there was security from the Viet Cong, both day and night, as compared with the 69 per cent at the end of 1968. The people in ever increasing numbers were providing information on the whereabouts and activities of the enemy—the rate at which this information was being volunteered was eight times greater than the previous year. Half a million people had enrolled in the People's Self-Defense Force. More and more the fighting had been pushed out beyond the populated areas. Rice production was flourishing; I saw thousands of hectares of the new Philippine strain of rice brought in by Americans to increase the output of Vietnamese paddyfields.

Local government was thriving and expanding. New hamlet and village officials, chosen in June 1969 by 89 per cent of the electorate, were fresh from government schools that provided special training to upgrade their administrative and service skills. These young public servants will be the backbone of the Vietnamese government for years to come.

There were still Viet Cong and grievous problems, but as I left Danang the last time, I saw the train once again puffing north to Hué along the repaired railroad track. It was a happy parting view, a portent for the future.

16

The Image
of War

The pretext of a National Liberation Front has been set aside by the enemy himself, and now we see his true nature. The remnants of the Viet Cong, bolstered by strangers from North Vietnam, lob rockets into Vietnamese towns. The uniformed regulars from the north try for mini-Dienbienphus at isolated outposts, while their comrades pour into Laos and Cambodia in new, bold aggression.

Such is the result, to the spring of 1970, of our first major confrontation with what Nikita Khrushchev named "Wars of National Liberation." It has tested us sorely in the field and at home, and tests us still. The enemy is no less implacable because he failed in Vietnam; instead, he has expanded the war to test us further. Nevertheless, the critical test was a War of National Liberation in its purest form, one in which every possible disadvantage weighed against us, a demonstration to all communists everywhere. For us to have failed this test would have encouraged the provocation of other such wars in Asia, the Middle East, Africa, and Latin America, as openly predicted in 1965 by Lin Piao, the National Defense Minister of Communist China, in his article "Long Live the Victory of the Peoples' War." That we did not fail will act as a restraint on

The Image of War

such wars until the communists can analyze their errors and change their techniques. What was hailed as a dynamic new form of warfare has soured. Now we find the frustrated forces of communism in open invasion of Laos and Cambodia, with no more pretense of "Peoples' War."

Our response to the challenge of Wars of Liberation has not accepted the mystique of "revolutionary warfare" as celebrated by so many writers. Neither has it adhered to that hypothetical rulebook military men are commonly accused of following blindly. We have blundered at times, and never were as brilliant as our critics. But I have found in fighting three wars that they are won by the side that makes the fewest mistakes and is flexible enough to learn the most from them.

American conduct of the struggle in Vietnam has its own quota of frustrations, but not nearly as many and as crucial as those suffered by the enemy. He has seen his vaunted doctrine of guerrilla warfare fail. He has been unable to topple the government of the Republic of Vietnam militarily or politically, and his resort to overt invasion—premature by his own revolutionary rulebook—was defeated in Vietnam. What is perhaps most galling to the communists is their having to revert, in Southeast Asia, to war with regular forces, while we Americans have been especially effective in the political area, in which we were expected to be the most ineffectual.

It is a truism that revolutionary war is fundamentally political, fought for political objectives with political weapons. The thoughts of Chairman Mao, the late Che Guevara, General Giap, and other theorists of communist conquest are devoted primarily to the political aspects of the wars they inspire and manipulate. That, however, is precisely where Hanoi was unsuccessful in South Vietnam. By this time it can be recognized as the major miscalculation of the late Ho Chi Minh and his foreign confederates.

They have failed to *transform an aggression into a civil war.*

The Image of War

That is the substance of their political defeat. They began with the claim—standard wherever communists plan a takeover by proxy—that the Viet Cong represented an internal rebellion. But they could not make it stick. There are still Americans who insist that it is a national or civil conflict. The Vietnamese, North and South, know better.

What little national character the Viet Cong may have had during their peak year of 1965 was fading by the end of 1966. This image was irreparably degraded by the invasion of regular forces from North Vietnam. When these regular soldiers from the north assumed guerrilla functions in the south, it made a mockery of the Viet Cong as a nationalist movement.

There has been no civil rebellion in Vietnam since the French departed. No margins of doubt remain that the present war in Vietnam was planned, launched, supplied, and controlled by Hanoi. It almost worked. The massive propaganda and savage coercion to which the people of Vietnam were subjected in early 1965 did not convince them politically, but it effectively withdrew all political choices except one: the Viet Cong. Later, when they were given the opportunity of choice, they did not rally to the Viet Cong in numbers sufficient to sustain them as a viable political movement.

But the Viet Cong never had the popular character of the original anti-colonial Viet Minh. The masses did not identify with or join them except under duress. Neither the insurgents nor the forces from the north would acknowledge this all-important difference between the First Indochina War against the French and the present war. They held to the delusion of a "united front" against "foreign imperialism," neither of which, in fact, existed. This was the delusion on which they counted in making the Tet offensive, at the end of which they had no reason, other than habit and the lack of an alternative, for clinging to it.

The idea that the United States became involved in a civil

The Image of War

insurrection has been propagated not only by Hanoi but by the communists and their partisans everywhere. In our own country, this claim has been accepted by a segment of the population, despite overwhelming evidence to the contrary. Once a person is persuaded that the war in Vietnam is a civil war, he has an honest rationale for backing away from U.S. commitments related to aggression. Official Washington, however, has witnessed too many other communist incursions on foreign soil, similarly disguised as local uprisings or revolutions, to be taken in by this one.

All administrations, beginning with that of President Eisenhower, recognized quite early that the threat to the independence of South Vietnam was external, not internal. Only a few months after the adoption of the Geneva Accords, President Eisenhower defined the danger as "attempted subversion and aggression through military means." On June 1, 1956, a young Democratic Senator, John F. Kennedy, publicly urged help to South Vietnam, which, he warned, "every day faces the growing peril of Viet Minh armies across the border." Five years later, as President, Kennedy wrote to President Diem in Saigon: "Our own information has convincingly shown that the campaign of force and terror now being waged against your government is supported and directed from the outside by the authorities in Hanoi."

Everything that happened after the Americans intervened in force confirmed that judgment. On the basis of documents, films, letters, and diaries captured from the Viet Cong, *U.S. News & World Report* (April 3, 1967) concluded: "So-called National Liberation Front turns out to be only a façade for Hanoi's Reds. The NLF issues no orders in the south, has no chain of command, military or political, no real power in South Vietnam." General Westmoreland told a joint session of Congress in 1967: "In three years of close study and observation, I have seen no evidence to the contrary—documented by the enemy himself—that it is simply aggression from the north."

In the earlier years there was the possibility that the struggle, though initiated and controlled from without, might be transformed into a national and civil war. In preventing this, American political good sense played a key part.

From the beginning we gave full recognition to South Vietnam as an independent, sovereign, and co-equal nation. We fought side by side with its armed forces as allies, advising but not directing. We assisted in the creation of a new government based on the will of the people. We respected the people, appealed to their interests, and steadily won their support, both for our presence in their country and for their own government.

We supported the South Vietnamese, organized a large local militia, encouraged a lenient policy on the rehabilitation of former Viet Cong, and we accepted losses ourselves in order to reduce those of the civilian population. With our aid, sometimes on our initiative, the social conditions that were the source of anti-government sentiment were progressively eliminated at the rice-roots level and at the national level.

As late as 1966 the Viet Cong might still have retrieved some political strength among the people by facing up to the new circumstances created by the infusion of American military might. They would have had to abandon some of their military gains, carry out a reduced guerrilla campaign from bases in the mountains, and, above all, give up their terrorism, assassinations, kidnappings, confiscations, and forcible conscription. They did none of these things. The error we were expected to make—that of allowing military considerations to outweigh the political struggle—was made instead by the enemy.

At no time could we have been evicted from Vietnam except by a real national front: the people against us as they had been against the French. The most desperate gamble of the war, the Tet offensive, was toward that end. The enemy threw all of his force, including the guerrillas, into an all-out effort to overthrow the government of the Republic. Having swallowed his own propaganda, he looked to a great tide of popular support.

In spite of our own prophets of doom, the Vietnamese people—during that offensive and more so after its failure—supported their government against North Vietnam and its Viet Cong auxiliary. They proved it in the month of crisis when the enemy flag flew over the ancient Citadel of Hué and fighting rocked the streets of Saigon. The Viet Cong had been pushed into committing the cardinal sin of the guerrilla: open, conventional battle with regular forces. Whatever remained of Viet Cong prestige was ruined, and the guerrilla remnants became, in effect, adjuncts to the North Vietnamese Army.

In the light of their national history it was to be expected that the people at first would regard the Americans as colonial invaders. They were conditioned by their unhappy experience. At one point I was worried whether it was credible to the Vietnamese that the United States, pouring blood and treasure into their country, building massive installations that could last a hundred years, would ever depart on their own volition. The worry evaporated sooner than I had hoped.

Fortunately we were not alone in South Vietnam. There were engineer units and civic action teams from the Philippines and thousands of soldiers from Korea, Australia, and Thailand. The story that these groups could tell—and we know that they did—refuted the assumption that Americans were "colonialists." They told how Americans had come to countries in their time of deepest trouble, had died for their cause, had constructed great airfields, ports, bridges, and roads—and departed when the job was done, leaving behind another beachhead for freedom.

The Vietnamese became aware of these facts, and they noted

that Americans rarely took on the manners and the arrogance associated in the Vietnamese experience with colonial conquerors.

Now we are seeing neighboring nations and peoples drawn into the struggle imposed so long on the Vietnamese people. The "domino theory" is obviously taken much more seriously in Southeast Asia than by some of our pundits at home. The strong cement of American-Vietnamese cooperation having firmly anchored one of the dominoes, the enemy appears to be testing some of the others. I have often thought that those who sneer at the "so-called" domino theory should question one of the dominoes. Ask the Burmese and the Thais about what would happen if the Republic of Vietnam became a communist state. Ask the Indonesians or Malaysians. Ask the people of Singapore; ask the Laotians and Cambodians. All of these peoples live under the same threat of becoming Asian Czechoslovakias.

The mere presence of Americans in Vietnam raised the morale of countries living in the shadow of Red Chinese power. The Foreign Minister of Thailand, Thanat Khoman, was speaking for all noncommunist leaders in Eastern Asia when he said, a few years ago, "If the Americans succeed in Vietnam, there will be no second Vietnam, no third Vietnam." Our own leadership, through four Republican and Democratic administrations, has recognized the threat to free nations in Southeast Asia, and our obligations and interests there.

The Southeast Asia Mutual Defense Treaty (SEATO), approved almost unanimously by the Senate, explicitly pledged the use of "appropriate means" to meet any threat to the sovereignty of South Vietnam. Military as well as economic aid to the Saigon government has been voted year after year since 1955, and each time Congress attested that the purpose was to fortify it against the mounting communist threat. On October

The Image of War

25, 1960, President Eisenhower, having noted this threat, offered assurances that "for so long as our strength can be useful, the United States will continue to assist Vietnam in the difficult yet hopeful task ahead." President Kennedy repeated this promise in stronger terms a year later, condemning "the deliberate savagery of the communist program of assassination, kidnapping, and wanton violence."

On August 10, 1964, a joint resolution of Congress, with only two opposing votes, authorized the President to "take all necessary steps . . . to prevent further aggression," and specifically listed "the use of armed force" among the "steps." Five years after its passage, questions are being raised about the Tonkin Gulf episode that prompted the resolution. No questions can be raised, however, about the crisis in Vietnam at the time and the desperate plea of Saigon for American assistance. Long years before the Tonkin resolution, communists under Hanoi's direction had been harassing American civilian and military installations in Vietnam, bombing American offices, assaulting and kidnapping American personnel. Short of walking out on a major national commitment, U.S. intervention was inescapable, whatever the second thoughts about Tonkin Gulf.

Those who say that we "rushed" into Vietnam are distorting history. Though the North Vietnamese aggression had been under way since 1954, U.S. forces in South Vietnam stood at only twenty-three thousand ten years later, at the end of the critical year 1964. Not until early 1965, when a complete communist takeover appeared imminent, was a genuine buildup of U.S. power undertaken. Thereafter, too, the process of involvement was slow and reluctant. History may blame us for not bringing adequate military potential to bear at once, instead of spreading it thin over a period of years. The fact is that every enlargement of U.S. military action has been a specific and measured response to escalation by the enemy.

As in any other foreign-policy decision, there is always room for argument about its wisdom. Hindsight operates in all fields of human decision. But certainly there is no room for denial that the commitment in Vietnam existed, assumed at the highest levels of government and consistently supported by Congress. Moreover, it has acquired an overarching moral dimension. Ever since 1954, American pronouncements, promises, and actions have encouraged the South Vietnamese to persevere in resisting communism. To leave them at the mercy of the enemy would therefore have come close to a moral betrayal. In President Johnson's words, "A just nation cannot leave to the cruelties of its enemies a people who have staked their lives and independence on America's solemn pledge."

In the preceding chapter I have summed up the truly dramatic progress achieved in Vietnam: security against Viet Cong depredations for 93 per cent of the people, erosion of North Vietnam's military strength, wider and more confident local government, improved economic conditions, especially in the production of rice.

Why, then, the pessimistic "image" of the war in so many American minds? We have been in other protracted wars that have produced some opposition at home, but none on the scale of this one. Even the Korean conflict, in the same general area and similarly "undeclared," did not arouse so much or such violent dissidence at home. Obviously there are elements that make the present war different.

One of them is that for the first time in history war has been brought into the living room of the ordinary American, with sensitive response to every tremor of the conflict through the machinery of modern communications. Prior to my return home in June 1967, I thought that this would make the citizen almost as well informed as myself; that it would close the gap between the returning soldier and his own people. Instead, I found many Americans frustrated and confused, filled with

The Image of War

fear, their image of the war something seen dimly through a distorted lens. Yet never in three wars had I seen so much coverage by the news media, such untrammeled liberty of expression, such freedom to travel about the war zone, or such opportunities to record the conflict by word, picture, and sound.

I have known and respected the profession of journalism for thirty years, and enjoyed the friendship of many top war reporters: Dick Tregaskis in those unforgettable days on Guadalcanal; Marguerite Higgins, charming even in shapeless GI fatigues, watching and writing of American men in the hills of Korea; Jim Lucas, Keyes Beech, all old friends, all professionals.

I met some of them again in Vietnam, along with new faces and new friends. They were still the press corps I had always known, men and women without illusions and without cant. They spoke and wrote the truth as they saw it. These were mature journalists who had shed their naïveté back in their cub reporter days. They could sort rumor from fact, spot propaganda in a moment, and were saddened but not shocked by the hard realities of war.

This association with professional journalism made it all the more perplexing when I encountered the disturbing lack of knowledge among the American people of what their sons were fighting against in Vietnam, and what they were accomplishing there. My concern on this score was shared by many respected members of the press corps, a number of whom had criticized their own profession for its reporting from Vietnam. It is not my place to join in this criticism, but it does seem to me significant that such men and women as S. L. A. Marshall, Maggie Higgins, Al Webb, Joseph Alsop, Frank McCulloch, Robert Shaplen, and Howard K. Smith have seen fit to criticize in varying degrees.

It *is* my place as a citizen—and one who has seen the war

[189]

both from the scene of action and from the United States—to be concerned about new conditions that operate to build up so confused a picture of so vital an event.

During my service in Vietnam more than five hundred accredited correspondents were in Vietnam. They ranged from seasoned war reporters to young men and women who had never published anything commercially. I was astonished to learn that anyone with letters from some newspaper or magazine offering to print his material could obtain accreditation as a correspondent from our own and the Vietnamese government. I encountered housewives and college students, adventuresome young girls, retired military men getting their last whiff of gunpowder, and other such free-lance writers and photographers among the "correspondents," traveling by government aircraft, requiring and getting protection and accommodations as they roamed the country.

But the war in Vietnam is not a simple one in which we seek only to find, fix, and destroy another uniformed force. Economic and social considerations are fundamental to the conflict; political and psychological factors are often more significant than military events. An understanding of what is transpiring is an interdisciplinary exercise, calling for broad knowledge, experience, and maturity. Rarely if ever before has the challenge to the war correspondent, in words and pictures, been more demanding.

From the military viewpoint most of the actual combat (60 to 70 per cent) is at night; half of the remaining engagements, those taking place in daylight, are small-unit actions. These are dangerous, tightly disciplined, meticulously planned activities, wearying and monotonous. They are not "news"; they are, however, 85 per cent of the fighting.

The remaining 15 per cent is that small fraction sufficiently dramatic to elicit headlines and in sufficient natural light to permit television coverage. Even here, the subject matter is exceedingly narrow, viewed largely from what the fighting man considers the rear: the helicopter landing site, the command post, supply dumps, perhaps an artillery battery in action. This is war seen through a peephole in the backyard fence.

I do not contest the views of correspondents who come to Vietnam hating war in general and the Vietnam war in particular. I am concerned about the amateurism of a small number of them. I doubt whether any man has hated war more than Ernie Pyle did, or reported it with greater wisdom and compassion. Not every man can be a great reporter, but he can be more than a poor one or a biased one.

Free-world photographers and television teams, of course, are denied all access to the Viet Cong and North Vietnamese side of engagements, battles, sieges. As a result the *visual* reports reaching our people at home depict primarily the death and anguish and destruction suffered by our men, our planes, our installations. The losses sustained by the enemy, though many times greater, may be reported in words, but they are rarely *shown*. This one-sided camera reporting is unavoidable, but it further contributes to an unbalanced view of the Vietnam war.

Day after day we read about and view the suffering of our own men and the South Vietnamese, the fatigue and the despair, the dead and the wounded. However unintentionally, the false impression is thus pounded into the public mind that the costs to our side are vastly greater than to the enemy.

I recall the image of the long fight in and around Khe Sanh: dirty, tattered infantrymen cleaning the muck off their rifles, collapsed in exhaustion, hugging the ground under fire. These were the men who in conjunction with South Vietnamese soldiers and supported by our strong air arm, killed twelve thousand regular North Vietnamese soldiers; who, in seventy-seven days of unending combat, lost exactly two hundred and five Marines. How did it appear at the time through our own news media, to the families of the men at Khe Sanh? I know how it looked to me, though I knew what the real situation was: it looked as if our men were trapped in a desperate siege, suffering and dying, and fighting to the last man.

In all those seventy-seven days one C-130 transport plane was destroyed on the airstrip by enemy shelling. Day after day I saw *the same aircraft* used as a backdrop for the action around the airfield and photographed on television, from every conceivable angle. Smashed, charred, it was always a dramatic shot. To the average viewer, I am sure, it seemed each time to be another and yet another of our planes torn up by enemy fire, mute symbol of the hopelessness of our plight in Khe Sanh. This may be art, but it is not reporting.

Newspapers, wire services, networks, and magazines send some top-flight journalists to Vietnam, competent reporters who apply themselves to understanding the war as it is, through hard work, danger, and disease. Some of them die doing it: Dickey Chapelle, on a patrol with the Marines; Dr. Bernard Fall killed by a Viet Cong mine on the "Street Without Joy" about which he had written so superbly; Maggie Higgins, ravaged by tropical disease contracted where she had always found her great stories—down among the squads and platoons, in the paddies and the hills. There are ever so many others, heard and read in the United States. The television crews are magnificent in their competence and heroic dedication to their dangerous work, and many of them have paid with their lives.

Mine is no plea for censorship, unless it be within the profession of journalism itself. My feeling is that actually much of what happens in Vietnam is now "censored," in effect, not by governmental machinery but by the incapacity of some reporters to see and report more clearly and in better context. It is not a matter of assessing blame, but of understanding the reasons for misleading emphasis, to the point of distortion, no less harmful because it is unintended.

The Image of War

A relentless theme in our media has been the suffering of the Vietnamese people at our hands, at the hands of our allies. There is no doubt of the magnitude of that suffering. We and the South Vietnamese are blamed for it. Yet we know that the war was imposed on South Vietnam by Ho Chi Minh and his government, with decisive material support from Communist China, Soviet Russia, and some of the Warsaw Pact countries. The suffering of the Vietnamese people is thus the direct result of communist aggression. In the measure that the suffering is blamed on the defenders, rather than the instigators, it seems to me that the war is being misrepresented.

It is my contention that in a war of this type, where the battle is as much in the psychological and political arena as on the battlefield, members of the news media have a special obligation. Objective reporting of this war has become more than an accurate accounting of what is seen and heard; it has become an exercise in mature judgment to be sure that the reports do not contribute to Hanoi's effort to manipulate world opinion. The news media in our country must continue to be free of government direction, but they must be free also of influence from nations or factions whose objectives are inimical to the United States.

Our forces in Vietnam have been undefeated in any major engagement in five years of fighting. There has been hardly a war of the United States in which we did not meet initial defeats: the Kasserine Pass, Bataan and Wake Island, and Taejon. We have experienced no such defeat in Vietnam, but we have suffered psychological defeats in the United States instead.

Our military success is to the honor and credit of the superb young Americans who have served and sacrificed in Vietnam, but I have not seen or heard this significant fact mentioned on the printed page or on television. Instead, when one of our outposts is attacked it is often reported as if it were another

The Image of War

Dienbienphu; when an enemy unit is trapped and destroyed, it is often reported as if the action were a senseless sacrifice of our men for a useless piece of ground.

The appalling innocence of giving national and worldwide distribution to enemy propaganda is another curiosity of the Vietnam war worth mentioning. American media, of course, realize that any release from Hanoi is propaganda. But surely, it seems to me, there should be more restraint and prudence in using them. They come from a communist source more rigidly controlled than Nazi Germany. Naturally, the forces of North Vietnam and the Viet Cong are portrayed as stalwart, confident, brave, clever, idealistic. Our newspapers and magazines are careful to identify the source of this "news." Yet the total impact of their propaganda messages registers on the reader's and viewer's mind.

The same week these words were written, for example, a national press service distributed a photograph made available by Hanoi. It shows a captured American, a huge man, his head down, a picture of utter dejection, guarded by a tiny and smiling Vietnamese girl whose head comes only to his elbow. This appeared widely in our morning and evening papers; one of the captions said that it was the most popular in a Hanoi display of war photographs.

It was not news. Neither the American nor his cheerful girl guard was identified. We were not even told when or where the photograph was taken. It had, however, a powerful psychological message: "American strength and power is a sham. See the tiny girl with this great brute under her control. This is the way the war will end, America head down and dejected, North Vietnam smiling and confident." No one can question the right of the press to publish it—only the wisdom of doing so. A few such propaganda confections may do no harm, but their cumulative effect, when presented month after month, year after year, is another matter.

The Image of War

We are engaged in a battle of words and pictures no less important than the battle of men and firepower, and it is one for which we are grossly unprepared. Advertently or inadvertently, our prodigious coverage of the war has influenced the attitude of the American people and other peoples of the world. Increasingly in the last few years the reporting has encouraged an atmosphere of hopelessness and futility, although there has been great and increasing room for hope.

Compare our image through our own mass media with that of the enemy. There are no pictures of tired Viet Cong or bodies of North Vietnamese invaders, or exhausted men and weeping women on the enemy's side. The image of the war conveyed to the American people has been through a curiously narrowed lens. The suffering shown has been our own, the brutality perpetrated by us, the horror somehow our responsibility.

It was Ho Chi Minh who started the war and let loose a ferocious terror against the South Vietnamese people. Why, then, has he been represented by some writers and speakers as a saintly uncle, while our leaders are castigated for their war actions? Why is Vo Nguyen Giap exalted as a brilliant military leader, with no mention of crushing defeat at our hands in the prime area of his proclaimed genius: guerrilla combat? It is Giap, not Westmoreland or Abrams, who is fumbling futilely with divisions of regular troops, his own lessons of guerrilla warfare abandoned, and being defeated in the field. Why is the reckless use of flamethrowers and the lobbing of explosive rockets into civilian communities by the enemy so blithely accepted as legitimate warfare by the American public? Why must the invasion of Laos and Cambodia by a hundred thousand communist troops be reported with cool objectivity, while the seizure of communist war supplies in those same countries by American and Vietnamese soldiers is greeted with editorial anguish and the implication that the United States has escalated the war?

The Image of War

It is easy to say, "War is bad, peace is good." No one denies that in principle. But there are worse things than war, and one of these is tyranny. I am a professional soldier but I am also a free man from a free country. I have fought tyranny all my life: the tyranny of militarism; the tyranny of oppression and subjugation; the tyranny of fascism, the tyranny of communism.

It was an American general who said that "war is hell," and we all subscribe to that judgment. But our armed opposition to tyranny and oppression has been the means of ending inhumanities greater than the armed conflict itself. Without such armed opposition, Hitler would still be stuffing Jews into ovens at Belsen and Dachau; without it today some 17 million Vietnamese would now be enduring what the population of Hué endured in one murderous month of communist occupation—and we haven't uncovered all their bodies yet. Men willing to fight against tyranny, willing to stand the long watches on the Ben Hai River, have spared millions of other Vietnamese people this horror. They held the tyrants back so that a free nation could be built and, hopefully, they arrested the tide of conquest threatening to engulf all of Southeast Asia.

17

Summing Up

Our soldiers, sailors, Marines, and airmen now returning from Vietnam need make no apologies for having largely stamped out terrorism and pushed back the invading hordes of communism. They can be proud of the millions of refugees to whom they have given shelter, the civilian millions whom they have fed and clothed and provided with medical care, the young generation to whom they have given an opportunity to be educated for life in a free society.

This is true despite what happened in My Lai two years ago. What I have to say about such events does not imply condonation of crimes committed on the field of battle. Those of us who pioneered in civic action to raise the human dignity and improve the lot of the Vietnamese people are especially horrified by reports of American depredations. American policy and American instinct have been geared to compassion, restraint, and sympathetic cooperation with the people.

I know of no major crime in Vietnam in which the Americans involved had not been exposed to many hours, days, or weeks of the most grueling strain. With negligible exceptions they occurred in areas controlled by the enemy. The grinding tension of long combat under constant threat of sniper fire, the

[197]

Summing Up

sudden explosion of a mine or booby trap, the hostility of villagers under the eye of murderous Viet Cong or North Vietnamese cadres—these can hardly be grasped from the armchair of an American living room. The remarkable fact is not that a few men succumb to the bestiality of reprisal, but that it happens so seldom. Within my personal knowledge, there have been fewer than a dozen incidents involving Marines in anything approaching "atrocity" during the five years of fighting by some six hundred thousand Marines in Vietnam.

The 2 million Americans or more who have been in Vietnam—all young, all armed, homesick, subject to sudden death or mutilation—are equivalent to a very large American city. Every newspaper reader knows that the incidence of murder, rape, and other crimes committed by individuals in a city that size, in normal peacetime conditions, is much higher than that reported in Vietnam.

Such aberrations are severely punished, whether in civilian life or in the fighting forces. In my opinion, they do not justify sweeping condemnation of our men in uniform as a whole, any more than of civilian society as a whole. If the conduct in My Lai has been concealed or blurred, deliberately or otherwise— at this writing the facts are not all in—it is a shocking exception, and certainly not typical. I know from personal experience that criminal acts in Vietnam are dealt with firmly, in sorrow and disgust, and the guilty punished within the framework of the law.

I have followed the massive reportage, day after day, on the real or alleged misconduct of one American soldier or Marine or American unit. Not in mitigation but in terms of reality, it should be said again that the communists engage in unlimited terror against noncombatants *as a policy*. The murder of thousands of innocents in Hué during the 1968 Tet offensive was not an incident but a deliberate communist strategy of extermination. The enemy has slaughtered tens of thousands—teachers, priests, police officers, local leaders and their families—and kidnapped even larger numbers during the past fifteen years. He deliberately hurls rockets and fire-bombs at random into crowded cities, movie theaters, schools, markets. He has committed crimes with calculated savagery, such as public beheadings, disembowelings, and maiming of innocent victims.

We had half a million men in Vietnam at the peak of our military effort. They battled an enemy of freedom, and at the same time battled disease and privation, desolation and despair. Their victories have less to do with "body counts" than with security and a helping hand given a suffering and deprived people. Happiness, health, and hope, food and shelter for millions, hospitals, orphanages, and schooling for children, have been the fruits of their labor. We can be proud, not ashamed, of our young Americans.

The question closest to the hearts of the people I have talked to, of course, has been: When will the war end? I could only explain that it will end when the enemy abandons the attempt to seize control of the people of South Vietnam by force. We have never had the mission or the intention to destroy the communist regime in the North, but have been determined to prevent Hanoi from taking over the South. When that purpose is accomplished, the South Vietnamese people, with the aid of their allies, will have "won" the war as well as the peace.

If the enemy could bring themselves to admit it, the war was lost for Hanoi and its Viet Cong in February and March of 1968. At that time a communist military victory over the people of South Vietnam became most improbable; it was denied, in a large part, by the will of the people themselves.

Tragically, the fighting continues as the enemy tries to retrieve his losses, which are vastly greater than those on our side. The formula he applies is the same he used in Korea:

pressures on the battlefield and intransigence at the conference table. And this time he has added another ingredient: his hope of the erosion of the American will to remain in the struggle even on a reduced scale.

American opinion has been as much a target in this war as an enemy soldier in the sights of a rifle. We have known psychological offensives before, but on this scale it is something new to us, just as guerrilla warfare once seemed new. The camera, the typewriter, the tape recorder are very effective weapons in this war—weapons too often directed not against the enemy but against the American people. These weapons have a far greater potential for defeating us than the rockets or artillery used against our men in Vietnam. In a free society, in which the right of dissent is a sacred principle, an enemy has boundless opportunity to manipulate our emotions.

I have never believed, and do not believe now, that it is the will of the American people to abandon the Republic of Vietnam to communist imperialism. If that will is subverted, we shall have become the victim of propaganda as deadly and cynical as the worst Viet Cong terrorist.

Our men in the field have asked me more agonizing questions than any posed at home.

Those who think a commander's function is confined to the exercise of authority should accompany one to a field hospital. I know of no combat commander who does not do this, often daily, not as a duty but as an obligation to the men whose broken bodies are the price of battle. With few exceptions the spirit of the men, even the most grievously wounded, is a moving and humbling experience. Their first questions are about their buddies and their units. They retain the winning spirit they had in battle even as the plasma drips into their open veins. Most commonly, their next concern is not for themselves, but for the anguish their being wounded may bring to their loved ones at home.

Summing Up

With the rest of the American people I have watched with an aching heart as the score of American dead climbed to thirty thousand, to forty thousand. I know the spirit in which these men sacrificed their young lives.

Many years ago, before the days of evacuation by jet aircraft, we buried our dead in the battle area. I remember one such place, the long neat rows, each graced with all we had to grace it: a fresh palm frond. Over the entrance way someone had placed an inscription on a plain board: *"Here dead we lie, nor would we wish to live and shame the land from which we sprung."* The board has long since mouldered away. The men for whom these words spoke were brought home long ago. But I and others can never forget either the men or the words. We still regret those deaths, but we have no reason to regret what those men accomplished for our nation.

There is supposed to be a generation gap between me and the men I served with in Vietnam. I crossed it countless times each day, over a bridge of respect—not their respect for me, although I think I had it, but my respect for them. I didn't build that bridge: I found it there already, part of our nation's tradition and heritage.

Many times in the last year I have heard others refer with some pride to the thousands of young people who demonstrate against the war in Vietnam. Invariably they were unaware of —and quite astonished by—equally impressive figures of another kind of demonstration. I have cited them already in an early chapter, but they merit repetition in the present context:

• Some 42,000 Marines have demonstrated their loyalty and dedication to their country and to the cause of freedom by voluntarily remaining in Vietnam at the end of their normal tour of duty, for six months or more of additional service.

• Over 100,000 soldiers of the U.S. Army have chosen to remain overseas or have requested to go back after returning to their homes and country.

Summing Up

Theirs is a commitment, not for a walk in the sun and the chanting of mindless slogans, but at the risk of death or disabling injury. It is not for money or fame or promotion: it is an expression of identification with the great historic struggle in Southeast Asia and other parts of the world. They are a significant segment of our youth signifying that they know why they are in Vietnam. They have fought and stayed to fight further, because they believe in the dignity of free men with the instinct of free men. They are willing to fight for the freedom of others, though they know that such dedication is now treated with contempt by some elements in our population.

It is men such as these who formed the living shield that gave the people of Vietnam the chance—the certainty, if our resolution does not falter—to survive as a free and independent nation. That shield was given them first in 1965, when they were losing the will to resist after more than a decade of communist subversion and erosion. Today, in 1970, they are confident and determined, proud as they have always been, but with the increased pride of having met one of the greatest crises of their long history and overcome it with our help. Each day their capability of standing alone against the enemy threat grows. The people—not just the government—are organized in their own defense and will die with weapons in their hands rather than submit to communist bondage.

This is what more than forty thousand Americans have created by their personal sacrifice. Each young man returning whole from Vietnam owes his debt to those who died or who have been maimed for life. Each family that welcomes a loved one home owes its joy to those men who did not come home—and to more than a hundred thousand young Vietnamese who have made the same sacrifice, and to the ones who are now replacing our fighting men in increasing numbers.

The Americans who died in Vietnam, moreover, have given new hope to hundreds of millions in Asia that they too can

Summing Up

survive as nations without submitting to the yoke of communist tyranny. The strategy of conquest-by-proxy has been checked in a test case of the cynically miscalled "Wars of National Liberation." Vietnamese still unborn will remember those forty thousand and more, as the Korean people remember other Americans who died far from home, because Asians have a long memory.

These are some of the answers I give myself and the people I talk to, and the families and friends of those, living or dead, who have done their part in Vietnam. It has become unfashionable in some quarters, I know, to talk of patriotism and love of country. Along with the overwhelming majority of my countrymen, I am content to remain "unfashionable."

Events in Southeast Asia continue to churn. By the time these words are read, much will have happened as a result of the communist aggression in Laos and Cambodia. As of this moment, in mid-1970, there are only indications and surmises on the true direction of events.

The frustrated forces of communism may be turning to new aggression against weaker nations as an abandonment—even temporarily—of their long and grueling effort to destroy the Republic of Vietnam and capture its land and people. If the communist forces now flinch from the strength and resolve of a free people, our sacrifices have not been in vain.

The enemy can well be trying to restore his tarnished image by seizing or partitioning another of his weaker neighbors, in order to claim some victory from his defeat. Or, with the inflexibility of purpose so characteristic of a totalitarian system, he may be adhering to his long effort to bring down the government of Vietnam through the establishment of hostile border countries.

Will Vietnam stand firm in the face of this latest threat? I not only hope it will; I believe it will. If I am wrong, I know my sorrow will be shared by many others, and that among these will be the men and their families who once again will have to face the realities of "Wars of National Liberation," as long and terrible as the Vietnam war, in other arenas of the communists' choice.

Drums of propaganda are throbbing out their messages: the weakness and ineffectiveness of the Cambodians; their brutality against the Vietnamese; the communist victories and successes. There is small mention of who brought war to Cambodia, or of the forty thousand communist troops who have invaded the country.

The central theme has been to "Get out of Cambodia," and it has been a rallying point for many thousands of the innocent and uninformed. The real communist demand, lost in the furor of oratory, concealed under cloaks of peace and good will, has been this: "Give us back our sanctuaries!"

The people most concerned, the Cambodians, appear to have made their choice: defend their land against the invaders, and welcome support from the free nations.

Some of the observers on the scene in Southeast Asia have been sufficiently experienced to recognize the important fact that Cambodia would have been unable to change its policies on communist use of their territory as a sanctuary without the determined stand of the Vietnamese people against Hanoi's intrusion. They recognize that the majority of the Cambodian people are following the example of the Vietnamese because they believe North Vietnam has lost the war in the south. I subscribe to these views.

I also agree with those who see the current events in Southeast Asia as dangerous to communist objectives in that area. The loss of Sihanoukville as a port of entry, the denial of other ports and beaches on the southern coast of Cambodia and of the "Sihanouk Trail" leading overland toward Vietnam, sharply cut the flow of communist war material from overseas.

Summing Up

The seizure of vast quantities of guns, ammunition, and other essential supplies by American and Vietnamese troops in the previous sanctuaries of eastern Cambodia has been another serious blow to communist aggression in Southeast Asia. The roots and sap stems of their supply system have been torn and severed. The products of communist arsenals—brought into Southeast Asia at enormous expense and in the effort to wage war against free men—are now in the hands of free men to be used in their own defense against tyranny.

I agree too with those who point out that the invasion of Cambodia by North Vietnamese is a different kind of war from the initial subversion and invasion of South Vietnam. The Cambodians are an old and proud people, with their own language and a culture that goes back to the antiquities of Angkor Wat. By feature and by tongue the North Vietnamese are strangers in the Cambodian land. The communists in Southeast Asia could be losing, not regaining, a privileged sanctuary by the gamble they are now making.

The Cambodians have been close to the threat of communism for many years. Under Prince Sihanouk they tried to accommodate it but the issue is now clear to them: it is not enough only to survive; you must survive as an independent people. The Vietnamese in the south have learned this, and the Thais know it. So do the Indonesians, the Malaysians, and the men and women of the Philippines.

Whatever the fate of Cambodia, I think we have brought a new wind of revolution to Asia by our stand in Vietnam. It is the true revolution of free men against oppression. I do not know what its ultimate form will be, but I do not think it will be the false revolution of communism. In the long run Eastern Asia will stand against this most recent threat, and many more beyond it. Unless these people are utterly abandoned, the revolution they want will not die at the muzzles of Russian or Chinese guns in the hands of North Vietnamese communists. I think that Asian communism fears the revolution of freedom far more than they fear anything else they have ever known, for in it are the true seeds of their own destruction.

There is much more to tell than I have told, and I know others will tell it: the indomitable Marine aviators who risked their lives daily over Vietnam; the men of the fleet offshore and in the little craft along the coast; the mechanics and wiremen and supplymen who kept materials moving through hundreds of miles infested with mines and snipers. I wish I had the skill to put on paper the heat and fatigue, the interminable days and nights, the loneliness of each man in the midst of multitudes, the sorrow and indomitable will that was in each of us.

This has been in the first place a Marine's story about Marines, because that is what I know best. It has been focused largely on the five northern provinces of Vietnam, because that was my area of responsibility for two years and my main area of interest since becoming Assistant Commandant of the Marine Corps.

It is for these reasons that I have not gone on to give the full measure of credit richly deserved by all other services: the superbly professional Army, which fought its own hard battles in the paddies of the delta and in the Central Highlands; our great Navy, which not only ruled the seas but drove inland in small craft manned by rugged sailors, all the way to the Cambodian border; the superb proficiency and dedication of the aviators and airmen, both Air Force and Navy, who not only gave us every support, but did so with the ever present threat of the years of prison and maltreatment still suffered by men they knew and flew with; the United States Coast Guard, so far from our own shores, on their interminable watches off the coast of Southeast Asia.

It is not within my capacity to give adequate recognition to

Summing Up

our allies—the men from Australia and New Zealand, Korea and the Philippines and Thailand, and most of all, the resolute forces of the Republic of Vietnam, who have stood with us against the cynical and brutal despotism that has poured into the south from the north.

I cannot say that we have won until the bloodletting in Vietnam—in all of Southeast Asia—is done. I think we have won to such an extent that millions will be able to stand as free men within the community of nations. They will owe us no debt, in money or in allegiance. Their survival in freedom, and thereby the strengthening of freedom, will be our only reward.

Acknowledgments

I owe a personal debt of gratitude to many whose efforts made this book possible: Gen. Leonard F. Chapman, Jr., Commandant of the Marine Corps, encouraged my effort in writing this book; Col. Don P. Wyckoff, USMC (Retired), rendered invaluable assistance in preparing and editing the manuscript; Capt. John J. O'Connor, Chaplain Corps, USN, contributed his deep understanding of the men and issues of the war.

There are many more, too numerous to mention by name: the countless Marines—active, reserve, and retired —who gave their loyal support; and several distinguished members of the news media who furnished advice so generously. To all of them I am grateful.

About the Author

LEWIS W. WALT, a four-star general presently serving as Assistant Commandant of the Marine Corps, is a much-decorated veteran of more than thirty-five years, with many years of combat duty as an infantry leader in World War II, Korea, and Vietnam. He was born on a Kansas farm in 1913. He worked his way through high school and Colorado State University where he was captain of the football, track, and wrestling teams, was student-body president, and earned a degree in chemistry.

As a member of the ROTC and cadet colonel he was commissioned a second lieutenant in the Army Reserve upon graduation, but resigned that commission in 1936 to accept an appointment as a Marine second lieutenant. He completed Officers' Basic School at Philadelphia in 1937 and by 1966 had advanced to the rank of lieutenant general. He served as a platoon commander in the defense of the International Settlement in Shanghai and on Guam before the Second World War. He was a company commander on Guadalcanal and a battalion commander in the northern Solomon Islands and Pelelieu campaigns. In Korea he commanded a Marine regiment and was chief of staff of a division.

When American forces were committed to the Republic of Vietnam in early 1965, General Walt became the commander of the Third Marine Division and the Third Marine Amphibious Force, responsible for the northern quarter of the country, which included the vital enclaves of Chu Lai, Danang, Hué-Phu Bai, and the entire frontier of the Demilitarized Zone. In July 1967 he returned to Washington and on January 1, 1968 assumed the second-ranking post in the Marine Corps. He received his fourth star in June 1969. In his two-year tour in Vietnam, General Walt is credited with setting the pattern of "two wars in one"—aggressive fighting combined with pacification and reconstruction in the countryside. He has been highly decorated by both the United States and foreign countries. He is known among Marines as "the Marine's Marine."